Seven Statements from the **Christian Bible**

THAT JEWS SHOULD KNOW

ALFREDO CALDERON-RODRIGUEZ

WESTBOW
PRESS®
A DIVISION OF THOMAS NELSON
& ZONDERVAN

WestBow Press books may be ordered through booksellers or by contacting:

WestBow Press
A Division of Thomas Nelson & Zondervan
1663 Liberty Drive
Bloomington, IN 47403
www.westbowpress.com
844-714-3454

Because of the dynamic nature of the Internet, any web addresses or links contained in this book may have changed since publication and may no longer be valid. The views expressed in this work are solely those of the author and do not necessarily reflect the views of the publisher, and the publisher hereby disclaims any responsibility for them.

Any people depicted in stock imagery provided by Getty Images are models, and such images are being used for illustrative purposes only. Certain stock imagery © Getty Images.

Scripture quotations marked NHEB are taken from the New Heart English Bible. Public domain.

Scripture quotations marked KJV are taken from the King James Version. Public domain.

Scripture quotations marked WEB are taken from the World English Bible. Used by permission.

Scripture quotations marked DARBY are taken from Darby's Translation of the Holy Bible. Public domain.

Scripture quotations marked ASV are taken from the American Standard Version. Public Domain.

ISBN: 978-1-6642-9977-1 (sc)
ISBN: 978-1-6642-9997-9 (hc)
ISBN: 978-1-6642-9978-8 (e)

Library of Congress Control Number: 2023909884

Print information available on the last page.

WestBow Press rev. date: 07/19/2023

CONTENTS

INTRODUCTION

One of the most significant accusations against the Jewish people throughout history is that they were the ones who killed Jesus. "Christ-killers" was the shout of the ignorant mobs as they burned synagogues during the pogroms in Russia and anti-Jewish raids in Nazi Germany. In times past, we can attribute this to the difficulty ordinary Christians had accessing the Bible message, especially outside major urban centers. However, in a highly advanced society, like the illustrious German society in Hitler's era, people fell to the different political and religious pressures. Usually, political, ideological, or religious movements, to gain followers through populism, need to cover up their numerous defects by creating scapegoats. At other times, fear of those we consider different from those we believe we belong to is enough to trigger repulsion mechanisms. This happened to the Jewish population and other minority groups during the Nazi regime in Europe.

It is also important to know that the Christian Reform also occurred in Germany, leading to a split between Roman Catholicism and Protestantism. The primary influence in that split was a renowned Catholic priest named Martin Luther. Today, even though Martin Luther was a reformist in the sixteenth century, his influence still seems to affect some Protestants.

In our times, in the twentieth and twenty-first centuries, the vast majority of Jesus's followers have direct access to the Christian Bible at any time. Also, there is a lot of freedom of interpretation of its message; however, some Christians still participate or follow this anti-Semitic behavior and beliefs. Even the great reformer Martin Luther gravitated toward a rigid view against the Jewish people. In his book, *On the Jews and Their Lies*, he evidenced some heavy rejections toward the Jewish faith and culture.

In Judaism, the religious, social, and cultural expressions are so intertwined that sometimes it is difficult to point to any of them as the sole reason for the anti-Semitism. That is why, in the non-religious territory—say cultural, economic, and social—we can find different expressions of prejudice. In the area of conspiracy theories, a book named *The Protocols of the Elders of Zion* is a sample of this. This book relates a false complot to control the world by Jewish Zionist movements. This is not the only one, but it may collect the spirit of anti-Semitism in the secular world. It is good to know that the theories of conspiracy is a realm in which anti-Semitism is not the sole topic.

We also know that Jews are not the only human group subject to persecution. People have suffered persecution throughout human history for various reasons; however, along with Christians persecuted for their faith, Jews have been the only other oppressed human group associated with the Bible. But why have some Christian sectors been part of this doubtful engagement? Does the Christian Bible contradict the anti-Jewish preachings of these so-called Christian voices? Can the Christian Bible explain it?

The terrible Inquisition mainly occurred in the fifteenth and sixteenth centuries in Spain. This religious movement resulted from the ignorance of the message contained in the Christian Bible. Most of the Christian population believed and obeyed what most ruling clergies wanted. In Middle Age Europe, many rulers of the Church, motivated by religious and political intrigues, personal interests, and fears, acted accordingly. Ordinary people who usually participated in mobs and anti-Jewish revolts did not access the Christian scriptures. Alternatively, they did not have the freedom to interpret them personally. They also were moved by manipulation, religious fears, favors, and prejudices to reject the Jewish population.

Factors like not knowing or not understanding what the Christian Bible says about the Jewish people have been the terrible cause in all those eventualities. Ignoring the high importance that the Christian Bible grants to the Jewish people altogether with the Christian Church is perhaps one of the main factors that has helped to create all this hate and prejudice. This disengagement manifests in two ways—Christian to Jews, Jews to Christians.

To see what the Christian Bible says about the Jewish people, it is better to stay mainly on the "Christian side" of the Bible. It is good to use the New Covenant in different versions, even though the Old and New Testaments comprise a single and unified book from an evangelical point of view.

Also, the reason there are different versions of the Bible is not to force meaning but to reinforce the message of the Bible by using different ways to say the same thing. In our modern world, in the midst of the process of globalization that we are experiencing, the need for better coexistence has increased. The revolution in communications has made us so close that the great need to understand each other has grown exponentially.

However, the emphasis for the best translators of the Bible has been to stay within the original message. Their work was done according to the oldest manuscripts that are possessed without losing the fact that the message has to be understood by the human groups for whom the translations have been done. Repeating once more, the Christian Protestant Bible is composed of the Old Testament and the New Testament.

We may use the terms Jewish scriptures and Old Covenant for the Old Testament and the terms Christian scriptures and New Covenant for the New Testament. The reader may find these terms interchanged in this analysis.

Another essential thing to know is that the Bible that Jesus and His followers read, quoted, and preached was the Jewish scriptures.

The New Testament emerged later based on the letters circulated by the inner circle of followers of Jesus among the first Christian communities.

There are some matters the Jewish people may know about the Christian Bible in the following pages—some things that even some Christians may ignore or pay little attention to.

A BRIEF INTRODUCTION TO THE CHRISTIAN AND JEWISH BIBLES AND THEIR RELATIONSHIP

WHAT IS A CHRISTIAN BIBLE? In nominal Christianity, there are different versions of the Bible; some essential things are regularly shared among them. Three main divisions, Catholic, Orthodox, and Protestant, together with other subdivisions in titular Christianity, maintain their arrangements in shared biblical books and other unshared ones.

The most related to the purely Jewish scriptures is the Christian Protestant compilation in which exactly all the books in the Jewish scriptures are an essential component, just ordered differently. The Jewish Bible is considered first by the importance given to the different sections, and the Evangelical Bible is arranged mostly chronologically. Both classification methods have their merits, but ultimately, with the Bible being the word of God, every section is meaningful and interconnected with the others.

The importance of the emphasis on chronological analysis lies in the fact that we can see in the events the unfolding of God's redemptive activities through the ages; in other words, what happens first comes before what happens later. An example is Daniel's knowledge of the prophecy of the seventy years of Babylonian captivity. First, God revealed the details to Jeremiah. Then Daniel, believing it, cried out to God for its fulfillment. The reverse order has no logic whatsoever.

When we examine replacement theology (this is discussed in more detail in Statement 6), we see that the chronological analysis easily dismantles the argument that the Church has forever replaced Israel as God's people on earth.

The Jewish section in the Christian Bible is known as the Old Testament or Old Covenant in Christian circles. The other part is called the New Testament or New Covenant. Both sections in the Protestant Bible are inseparable, interlinked, and intertwined; they are made with the same fabric. Neither is complete without the other. For this book, we will use the selection of the Protestant Bible.

The obvious Christian standpoint of the relationship between the Jewish (Old Testament) and Christian (Old and New Testament) Bibles is the reality that, if we were to make the Old Covenant disappear, the New Covenant will remain suspended in the air without its foundation. It wouldn't even be called new because there would not be a preceding one. The New Covenant is preconceived and announced in the Old Covenant. Therefore, the Old already contained its seeds when the New Covenant came into being.

The same goes for the most relevant figure in the Bible, the Messiah. If Jesus had appeared out of nowhere, declaring Himself to Israel and the world that He was the awaited Messiah who would save humankind from its terrible fate, there would be no single point of reference from which to launch. Surely people would ask in confusion: Who are you saying we are waiting for? What is this that you are talking about? Instead, when Jesus first appeared, there were already in Israel many preconceived details about Him and high hopes for this long-awaited Messiah. The place of birth, the type of death, His tribe, and so much other information gathered in the Old Testament are just a few examples of this, especially His powerful ministry of restoration and salvation.

Moreover, in Jesus's time, there was great expectation of this much-needed Messiah. The Roman Empire was oppressing the Hebrew people politically, religiously, and culturally, creating significant social unrest. That is why this awaited Messiah was expected but dressed as a conquering king and not as a suffering servant. Only a few, with great difficulty at first, were able to see Jesus in his first coming as the Lamb of God provided to be sacrificed for the sins of humanity. But, from those few, a gigantic universal Church arose and continued to grow unceasingly until its future culmination in the following ages. That is why we can say in Christianity that Jesus is that bridge that joins both covenants.

The Old Covenant fulfills a process whose total and perfect culmination is still in our future in the New Covenant. Both covenants describe God's intervention with humanity, and both are embedded in human history simply because God is in our midst and wants to be known as present. God constantly demonstrates that he wants to be part of our lives in every way.

On the other hand, if anyone considers that the New Covenant prophesied in Jeremiah 31:31–34 has not yet occurred, its manifestation is still in the future and shrouded in mystery. However, how can this New Covenant be identified? What characteristics must it meet?

It must be inseparable from and interrelated and intertwined with the previous one; otherwise, Jesus will not be the One God promised in the Jewish scriptures, for He would not have that connection. For that reason, there will be no disconnect between the Old and the New, but a transition from one maturing into the other until it reaches its glorious culmination.[1]

It does not matter that some people may believe that the Messiah has not come as of now, and with Him, the establishment of this predicted New Covenant. If this is the case for some who do not yet believe, then the New Covenant they are waiting for must have the same characteristics of the New Covenant through which the followers of Jesus long to live. This is why both covenants have to be inseparable and made with the same fabric. Let us say again—inseparable, interlinked, intertwined, and made with the same cloth.

Jesus validates this vital interconnection with these words to His disciples after His resurrection. "He said to them, 'This is what I told you, while I was still with you, that all things which are written in the law of Moses, the prophets, and the psalms, concerning me must be fulfilled'" (Luke 24:44 WEB). Here we find that Jesus mentions his connection with the three divisions of the Jewish scriptures. In other words, the Jesus figure is all over the Jewish scriptures.

Also, Jesus said something about the Law of Moses in particular: "Don't think that I came to destroy the Law or the prophets. I didn't come to destroy, but to fulfill. For most certainly, I tell you, until heaven and earth pass away, not even one smallest letter or one tiny pen stroke shall in any way pass away from the Law, until all things are accomplished" (Matthew 5:17–18 WEB). Once this is settled, let us go to work.

Surprisingly, most of the time, complex problems have straightforward answers. Jesus never ceased to amaze his detractors whenever they wanted to put him in trouble. His simple solutions to the seemingly complicated questions his pursuers tried to catch Him always left them speechless. Jesus constantly went to the origins of the controversies, a fallen human heart.[2] More than once, He used a child among His disciples and said to them, "Most assuredly, I tell you, whoever doesn't receive the kingdom of God like a little child, he will in no way enter into it" (Luke 18:16 WEB). See also Matthew 18:3–5; Mark 9:37, 10:15; Luke 9:45–48; and Luke 18:17. Following His example, let us try to work this analysis the same way.

INSERTION A: THREE BIBLE HISTORICAL STAGES—FROM THE EXPULSION FROM EDEN TO THE RISE OF THE CHURCH

The purpose of this insertion is to see how the Church and Israel fit in God's redemption plans for humankind. It is a panoramic chronological view, a timeline map that will help insert this analysis in their proper spot in time and space. Understanding the importance of the chronological approach when studying the Bible is vital for better comprehending God's redemption activities. The end never goes before the beginning; otherwise, the narrative will not make sense. In this approach to the Bible, anyone can easily find a very structured plan for God's redemption. We can find an example of this analysis in Statement 6.

In the period between the expulsion from Eden to the beginning of the fulfillment of the Christian Church purpose, we can see three very well-defined stages[3] as follows:

Stage 1: After the Fall to Father Abraham

Notable events in this first stage:

1- The fall and expulsion of the first humans from Eden
2- The universal Flood and the repopulation of Earth with Noah's descendants
3- The Babel tower and the scattering of the inhabitants throughout Earth
4- God's choice to create a nation out of Father Abraham

In this stage, we find God dealing with individuals of faith. Some of them, but not all, were Adam, Cain, Enoch, and Noah. Then, after Babel, there was Father Abraham. The Bible does not say anything about religious institutions within this period but only mentions people who believed in God's existence. These biblical heroes condemned a fallen world full of disobedient people who rejected God. Examples are Abel offering God better sacrifices than his brother Cain; Enoch, who walked with Him; and Noah, who obeyed His voice.

Stage 2: From Abraham and the Origins of Israel to the Birth of the Church

Notable things in this second stage:

1- The rise of the Hebrew nation throughout the patriarchs Abraham, Isaac, and Jacob.
2- The development of the Hebrew nation with all the importance that this implies.
3- Jesus's birth in Bethlehem, His ministry, teachings, crucifixion, and resurrection.
4- The birth of the Church.

Let us call this stage, the period of Israel, obedience. God worked His redemptive process through the Hebrew nation. God founded His nation, beginning with the faith nested in one Gentile heart, Abram. God transformed this man from Abram to Abraham, and from him, God created a nation named Israel. The purpose was to reach and bless all families of the world. So, we know that the first Hebrew was a Gentile man. We can see God's plans to redeem humanity through the Hebrew nation with a threefold mission at this stage:

1- To be a body of priests to all the nations. [4]
2- To give the world the holy scriptures. [5]
3- To be the human recipient of the Messiah who is for all humankind. [6]

This period is when the holy scriptures came into being, and the prophets of Israel were spreading their message. Their patriarchs were slowly, step by step, building a nation against all the odds and through challenging times. The roots of monotheism were slowly growing, and the Mosaic Law was moving humanity far ahead of time. The Old Covenant was in growth, and the New Covenant was only in prophecies. The coming of the Messiah set the beginning of the end of this stage that finished with the birth of the Church.

It was a time when Israel was struggling to obey God, but for the Gentile nations, it was a period of total disobedience, a time of total idolatry. *Only in Israel was God following up His redemptive plans.*

But what happened with the Gentile nations meanwhile? Did God abandon the Gentile people in this period? The answer is no. The Apostle Paul wrote something very significant when referring to this possibility (Romans 2: 12–16 and 11:30–32). Also, in the Jewish scriptures, we see the purpose of God's when He lifted a Gentile to be the first Hebrew to bless all the families of the earth (Genesis 12:1–4). Something very interesting indeed!

Since then, Israel has been a nation like no other. There has never been a nation on the face of the earth that has developed such a unique culture. The Hebrew nation is very particular and singular. It started from its origins through a man selected by God and continued through the production of the Bible, its patriarchs, judges, and kings. Also, their prophets, tabernacle, temple, sacred writings, and history of survival are some of the things that make them so particular. However, the unique and specific relationship of God with Israel as a nation is the most outstanding of all the characteristics any country on earth has had. For some Hebrews, this is an onerous burden to bear.

We could say that God's love for Israel has been and is incredibly persistent and stubborn, even with the existence of the Church.[7] Probably nobody can express this thought better than a famous Jewish adolescent. Anne Frank wrote in her diary the following words:

> Who has inflicted this on us? Who has set us apart from all the rest? Who has put us through such suffering? It is God who has made us the way we are, bu it is also God who will lift us again. In the eyes of the world we are doomed, but if, after all this suffering, there are still Jews left, the Jewish people will be held up as an example. Who knows, maybe our religion will teach the world and all the people in it about goodness, and that's the reason, the only reason, we have to suffer.
>
> Otto H Frank, Mirjam Pressler,
> *The definitive edition. The Diary of a Young Girl Anne Frank* (Bantam Books) 258-59

Not long after she wrote this, thousands of surviving Jews and some non-Jews were liberated from Nazi concentration camps. Sadly, she did not survive the insane hatred of the Holocaust. Then, almost three years after that, Israel rebirthed as a nation! What was the religious or cultural reason that so many Jews suffered the Holocaust? It was just because they were Jews and all that this implied for those who hated them!

Stage 3: From the Church to the Fulfillment of Redemption

Notable things in this third stage:

1- The Church rises throughout the Jewish Messiah and Jewish apostles.
2- Gospel brought to all nations as a witness of the Christian faith through the preaching of its message.

3- Once the purpose of the Church has been fulfilled (fullness of the Gentiles), the next stage will be the whole restoration of the Hebrew nation. [8]

Let us call this stage[9] the period of Gentiles' *obedience*.[10] Jesus identified this stage as the one humanity is living right now. In this stage, the message of the Gospel spread to all nations right before the end times. The Church issues a daily role as God's people currently on earth. In contrast, the Jewish people as a nation, in a temporary wait, remain hopeful for a future national and total redemption. Let us look at what the Christian Bible says about this:

> This Good News of the Kingdom will be preached in the whole world for a testimony to all the nations, and then the end will come. (Matthew 24:14 WEB)

> For I do not wish you to be ignorant, brethren, of this secret—that ye may not be wise in your conceits—that hardness in part to Israel hath happened till the fulness of the nations may come in; and so all Israel shall be saved, according to as it hath been written, "There shall come forth out of Sion He who is delivering, and he shall turn away impiety from Jacob, and this to them is the covenant from Me, when I may take away their sins." (Romans 11:25–27 WEB).

STATEMENT 1: JEWS DID NOT KILL JESUS.

Let us begin with the most proclaimed "sacred" lie against the Jewish people: they were the killers of the Christian Messiah. As for this great excuse used to cover other obscure hate motives, let us quote the same Jesus as registered by the apostle John.

> Therefore, the Father loves me, because I lay down my life, that I may take it again. No one takes it away from me, but I lay it down by myself. I have the power to lay it down, and I have the power to take it again. I received this commandment from my Father. (John 10:17–18 NHEB)

It is essential to notice that John was a Jew from the Galilee and a disciple of a Jewish rabbi, Jesus. The last three years of Jesus's life were in the constant company of His body of more intimate disciples, John included.

To see the veracity of John's witness of his Rabbi life, let us investigate some of his writings. In them, he insists on the reliability of his testimony:

> In the beginning was the Word, and the Word was with God, and the Word was God. (John 1:1 NHEB)

> And the Word became flesh and lived among us, and we saw his glory, such glory as of the one and only of the Father, full of grace and truth. (John 1:4 NHEB)

> That which was from the beginning, that which we have heard, that which we have seen with our eyes, that which we saw, and our hands touched, concerning the Word of life. (1 John 1:1 NHEB)

> But when they came to Jesus, and saw that he was already dead, they did not break his legs. However one of the soldiers pierced his side with a spear, and immediately blood and water came out. He who has seen has testified, and his testimony is true. He knows that he tells the truth, that you may believe. (John 19:33–35 NHEB)

Note the emphasis of John, making it very clear that he was a participant and a personal witness in his narratives. In other words, he was not a secondhand witness, but a firsthand witness. John also evidenced the transfiguration of Jesus along with Peter and James (Mark 9:1–9). This made a strong impression on them. We have in John a faithful narrator of what he lived side by side Jesus.

Based on Jesus's words, the Christian Bible never accused Jews or anybody else of His death. He proclaimed that He came to die voluntarily because of the sins of all humankind. *It is historically accurate to say that the Jewish religious authorities, along with some of their followers, delivered Jesus into Roman hands to be crucified (Mark 10:33). But it is much more accurate to understand that He was the Lamb of God provided for the ultimate and perfect sacrifice.* So, His death was something that had to happen even though the Roman Empire with its justice system provoked Jesus's physical death. But as for God, it was a love sacrifice, and very much needed indeed.

The systems that govern this world were represented in the judgment that preceded Jesus's death. The powers that control the human heart—economic, religious, and political—were present in the trial of Jesus. Each of these powers is related to the unhealthy needs of a fallen human nature. Finding people who desire to gain and maintain control over other people and nations over other nations is effortless. Those were the things Jesus constantly struggled against. Those are the characteristics of what Jesus called "the world."

Those were the motives behind Jesus's death precisely because the message He proclaimed was against any oppression from the ones who rule over the powerless, regardless of whether they are Jews or Gentiles. Those worldly powers work either by deception or by force.

Both Jews and Christians establish that the payment for our sins is death (Genesis 2:27, Romans 6:23). So, if people can live without sinning, death will not have any power over them. If Jesus was tempted in everything but remained without sin, why did He die then? (Hebrews 4:15). Well, as the innocent Lamb was to be sacrificed in the place of the debtors, Jesus was sacrificed for us, taking our place on that wood. In this sense, it is appropriate to say that we all killed Jesus, both Gentiles and Jews alike, because we have all sinned (Romans 3:23). Isaiah chapter 53 is a living portrait of this perfect atonement.

In the events of His capture and Judas's treason, Jesus confirmed that He came to die and, in that way, fulfill the scriptures. This text confirms His words registered in the Gospel of Matthew. Matthew was also one of the inner circles of Jesus's disciples.

> While he was still speaking, look, Judas, one of the twelve, came, and with him a large crowd with swords and clubs, from the chief priests and elders of the people. Now he who betrayed him gave them a sign, saying, "Whomever I kiss, he is the one. Seize him." Immediately he came to Jesus, and said,

"Hail, Rabbi." and kissed him. Jesus said to him, "Friend, why are you here?" Then they came and laid hands-on Jesus and took him. And look, one of those who were with Jesus stretched out his hand, and drew his sword, and struck the servant of the high priest, and struck off his ear. Then Jesus said to him, "Put your sword back into its place, for all those who take the sword will die by the sword. Or do you think that I could not ask my Father, and he would even now send me more than twelve legions of angels? *How then would the Scriptures be fulfilled that it must be so?*" In that hour Jesus said to the crowds, "Have you come out as against a robber with swords and clubs to seize me? I sat daily in the temple teaching, and you did not arrest me. But all this has happened, that the Scriptures of the prophets might be fulfilled." Then all the disciples left him and fled. (Matthew 26:47–56 NHEB, emphasis mine)

Jesus's death was a single event that happened once and for all. Jesus's sacrifice collected all the meaning of the constant atonement and offerings of the Old Testament. In those, a clean animal was offered to cover with his innocent blood the sins of the debtor. Jesus came to cover with His sinless blood the sins of anyone who calls onto Him.

The epistle to the Hebrews contains a concrete accomplishment of Jesus's sacrifice as a fulfillment of the Jewish scriptures. Many other passages in the Christian Bible are also confirmations of Jesus's triple-stage mission:

1- Propitiation
2- Expiation
3- Redemption

Propitiation means that Jesus soothed God's righteous wrath toward us. Expiation is the price that was necessary to pay to repurchase us from sin. Redemption is the act of restoring our position as children of God. All are impossible without His death and confirmed with His resurrection!

But why must there be two messiah visits to earth? Well, the suffering servant so well described in Isaiah 53 was Jesus when He was first introduced to humankind. These three stages of Jesus's mission on earth were at His first coming. Nowadays, simultaneously as we await His expected second coming, the purpose of the Church is being fulfilled. Once the fullness of the Gentiles is completed, we will see the King of kings in all His splendor coming in the clouds at His return. He will reclaim what He conquered out from the darkness when He offered Himself in sacrifice as the Lamb God provided (Daniel 7:13, Matthew 24:30, Revelation 1:7, Hebrews 9:28).

Jesus is alive because death could not hold him! This also implies that nobody can accuse anybody of killing someone who lives forever!

The statement is this:

Jesus came to die willingly; it was necessary and vital for humankind's redemption. As nobody could take away His life, He offered it out of love.

Below are some other quotes from the New Covenant, every one of them deeply rooted in the Jewish Bible.

Jesus as the Lamb for Passover: 1 Corinthians 5:7

Jesus as the Lamb of God that cleanses the sins of
all men: John 1:29, 36; John 3:16; John 19:32–36
Jesus dies in our place: Romans 5:8, 1 Corinthians 15:3
In His death, He was lifted: John 3:14

STATEMENT 2: THE GOSPEL CAME OUT THROUGH THE JEWISH PEOPLE.

Right after the capture of John the Baptist and just as Jesus
finished His forty days of fasting and temptation in the desert,
Jesus began preaching the Gospel in Galilee. "Now after John
was delivered up, Jesus came into Galilee, preaching the gospel
of God" (Mark 1:14 ASV).

The term *Gospel*, which means "good news," has over time
been associated with a religious system that is separate, different,
and somehow disconnected from its Jewish roots. The Gospel is
not something any human institution can bottle and then market
with exclusive rights. The Gospel is the power of God to transform
everyone in need who seeks the Messiah in spirit and truth.

The reality is that Jesus came to offer something more than
a new religious order. He came to share with the world the most
excellent news: "namely, that God was in Christ reconciling the
world to himself" (2 Corinthians 5:19 WEB).

Imagine the joy of the Lord as He went all the way to begin the
proclamation of such great news. Finally, the whole world would
receive a hope beyond human and religious expectations! When
Jesus began his ministry after the temptation,[11] he went directly to
the region of Galilee, where he was raised.

Of course, it all must begin through the people who received the
holy scriptures that foretold that they should expect a savior. It all
began with the Jews, a nation that was in expectation of the Anointed
One, the One who would come forth from the House of David.

Alfredo Calderon-Rodriguez

for Salvation is of the Jews

Jesus went out from there and withdrew into the region of Tyre and Sidon. Behold, a Canaanite woman came out from those borders and cried, saying, "Have mercy on me, Lord, you son of David! My daughter is severely possessed by a demon!" But he answered her not a word. His disciples came and begged him, saying, "Send her away; for she cries after us." But he answered, "I wasn't sent to anyone but the lost sheep of the house of Israel." But she came and worshiped him, saying, "Lord, help me." But he answered, "It is not appropriate to take the children's bread and throw it to the dogs." But she said, "Yes, Lord, but even the dogs eat the crumbs which fall from their masters' table." Then Jesus answered her, "Woman, great is your faith! Be it done to you even as you desire." And her daughter was healed from that hour. (Matthew 15:21-28 WEB)

This event portrays how beautifully dramatic it is to have a personal encounter with Jesus's healing presence. What soothing and peaceful security it brings to the soul of those that call on Him. Let's see how this Canaanite woman called Jesus: "Son of David," she said. Wasn't she a Gentile pagan woman? How did she know of a Jewish Messiah? Well, indeed, she had been in contact with the Jewish culture of the time. But how is it that she placed her hopes in a non-Gentile figure? Simply put, an encounter between the fallen human nature and the divine redemption took place—a moment when despair met divine redemption.

No wonder a great Jewish rabbi,[12] who was so indescribably shocked at one point when the risen Jesus transformed his life, wrote to the Roman believers as follows:

> For I am not ashamed of the gospel: for it is the power of God unto salvation to everyone that believeth; to the Jew first, and also to the Greek. [The Greeks here as a representation for all Gentiles.] (Romans 1:16 ASV)

One specific day, Jesus entered into an interesting conversation with a woman from Samaria. Jews and Samaritans did not get together after the Samaritans' "contamination" with the Gentiles. In the eyes of the people from Juda, that contamination came after the Assyrians exiled and mixed Israelites with people from other nations. The Assyrians defeated the Northern Kingdom of Israel by 722 BC.

> The woman said to him, "Sir, I perceive that you are a prophet. Our fathers worshiped in this mountain, and you Jews say that in Jerusalem is the

place where people ought to worship." Jesus said to her, "Woman, believe me, the hour comes, when neither in this mountain nor in Jerusalem, will you worship the Father. You worship that which you don't know. We worship that which we know; *for salvation is from the Jews.* But the hour comes, and now is, when the true worshipers will worship the Father in spirit and truth, for the Father seeks such to be his worshipers. God is spirit, and those who worship him must worship in spirit and truth." The woman said to him, "I know that Messiah comes, he who is called Christ. When he has come, he will declare to us all things." Jesus said to her,*" I am he, the one who speaks to you."* (John 4:19–26 WEB, emphasis mine

This is an excellent reference to the importance of the Jewish nation in God's plan to redeem all humankind.

The statement is this:

The Gospel is not a religious invention of the Gentiles; it is the perfect plan of God in which the Jewish people have an important role. In Jesus's own words: "for salvation is from the Jews." (John 4:22 WEB) Jesus was referring to Himself because He came out from the Jews, from the House of David.

STATEMENT 3: AS JEWISH PEOPLE DO; CHRISTIANS MAY ALSO CALL ABRAHAM FATHER.

Although people from religions other than Judaism or Christianity may call Abraham "father" as equal, it is very proper for a Christian person to do so. Paul, the apostle, whom God designated to reach out to the Gentiles,[13] wrote to the Christians through the Church in Rome. He spoke about Israel, the Church, and the relation between them. His letter to the Romans is a masterpiece of all times in which we can find valuable information about national Israel and his continuous importance in God's activity reaching out for people.

> For this cause it is of faith, that it may be according to grace, to the end that the promise may be sure to all the descendants, not to that only which is of the law (Ethnic Israel), but to that also which is of the faith of Abraham (The Gentiles in the Church), *who is the father of us all.* As it is written, "I have made you a father of many nations." This is in the presence of him whom he believed: God, who gives life to the dead and calls the things that are not, as though they were. Who in hope believed against hope, to the end that he might become a father of many nations, according to that which had been spoken, "So will your descendants be." (Romans 4:16–18 WEB, emphasis mine)

It is very important to notice that is not faith in Abraham the person, but it is more about the kind of faith that Abraham developed by trusting in God during his life. In his life, Abraham went through ups and downs like any other human being on this earth, but what he experienced was an ever-increasing relationship with the Almighty.

What kind of faith would be that of Father Abraham, who pleased God so much? Reading the Christian Bible, we can understand why Abraham pleased God so greatly; he trusted and relied upon the Almighty. Because of that, Abraham has the privilege and honor to be called "friend" by God (2 Chronicles 20:7, Isaiah 41:8).

You will be Father

of Many Nations

> "And the scripture was fulfilled which saith, Abraham believed God, and it was imputed unto him for righteousness: and he was called the Friend of God" (James 2:23 KJV).

Abraham, the one who went to Moriah to offer Isaac in sacrifice, was not a religious fanatic but a man transformed by the grace of God. Abraham knew already who God was and had enough confidence in Him when he was asked for the sacrifice of Isaac, the son of the promise. Abraham spent time with God throughout his life. When this moment arrived, he was fully confident that Isaac would return alive with him. Abraham said to his servants, "Stay here with the donkey. The boy and I will go over there. We will worship and come back to you" (Genesis 22:5 WEB).

> By faith, Abraham, being tested, offered up Isaac. Yes, he who had gladly received the promises was offering up his one and only son, to whom it was said, "Your offspring will be accounted as from Isaac," concluding that God can raise up even from the dead. Figuratively speaking, he also did receive him back from the dead. (Hebrews 11:17–19 WEB)

As with Christian scriptures, Jewish scriptures never hide the human weaknesses of the people God calls for His service. Father Abraham is an excellent example of this. Along with his life, Abraham showed that he was a simple human with moments of great trust in God. With the help of the scriptures, we can understand that trusting in the God of Abraham, Isaac, and Jacob is vital and not expendable if we want to live eternity with Him.

> ## *The statement is this:*
>
> **Abraham's example in the process of building a relationship with God through faith is the reason that Christians can also call him "Father."**

STATEMENT 4: SHIMON (PETER) OPENED THE DOORS OF THE CHURCH TO JEWS AND GENTILES

A very Jewish man named Shimon, whom Jesus called Peter (from the Greek *petrus* and the Aramaic *cephas*, meaning stone), was commissioned by Jesus to open the "gates" of the Kingdom of Heaven to both Jews and Gentiles. The birth of the Church is understood as the beginning of the earthly activity of the followers of Jesus after his resurrection. In the book of Acts, we have a clear and detailed account of the day the Church was born. The Church, the universal body of believers, was raised by the ministry of Jesus and the work of the apostles.

From the initial day to the present day, Christ believers have comprised the Church. The Church's birth occurred during a very Jewish feast, the celebration of Pentecost or Shavuot. It happened fifty days after the Passover when Jesus offered his life as the Lamb of God to cover with His blood the sins of humanity. Also, for the term *Church*, we are not referring to any particular Christian organization that proclaimed themselves to be the real and only ones who represent Christ on earth. We will see more of this ahead.

With great enthusiasm, Jerusalem was filled with Jews and proselytes who came to the feast from all the surrounding countries.

In the book of Acts, written by Luke, we can find details of that day of Pentecost. Chapter two of Acts vividly describes what led some three thousand Jews and proselytes to become the first believers without Jesus being present in a human body. Thus, the Church came into being by the supernatural power of the Holy Spirit on that momentous day. Chapter two of Acts is deeply rooted in the Jewish scriptures, as Peter mentions in this initial preaching about the Gospel. He brings to the light of the New Covenant some prophecies from the book of Joel and the book of Psalms. Those prophecies were fulfilled that day.[14]

> Now when the day of Pentecost had come, they were all together in one place. Suddenly there came from the sky a sound like the rushing of a mighty wind, and it filled all the house where they were sitting. Tongues like fire appeared and were distributed to them, and one sat on each of them. They were all filled with the Holy Spirit, and began to speak with other tongues, as the Spirit gave them the ability to speak. Now there were dwelling in Jerusalem Jews, devout men, from every nation under the sky. When this sound was heard, the crowd came together, and were bewildered, because everyone heard them speaking in his own language. They were all amazed and marveled, saying, "Look, are not all these who speak Galileans How do we hear, everyone in our own native language? Parthians, Medes, Elamites, and people from Mesopotamia, Judea, Cappadocia, Pontus, Asia, Phrygia, Pamphylia, Egypt, the parts of Libya around Cyrene, visitors from Rome, both Jews and proselytes, Cretans and Arabians: we hear them speaking in our tongues the mighty works of God." They were all amazed,

and were perplexed, saying one to another, "What does this mean?" Others, mocking, said, "They are filled with new wine." But Peter, standing up with the eleven, lifted up his voice, and spoke out to them, "You men of Judea, and all you who dwell at Jerusalem, let this be known to you, and listen to my words. (Acts 2:1–14 NHEB)

Then those who received his word were baptized. There were added that day about three thousand souls. (Acts 2: 41 NHEB)

We can observe that the purpose of a key is to allow entry into a particular place; in this instance, it is the Kingdom of Heaven in its new body of believers, the Church. The Lord Jesus chose Peter to handle the keys to open the doors of the Church initially to the Jews.[15] Peter opened the doors of the Church to Jews and proselytes on a momentous day. He inaugurated the era of the Church with a bold message on that particular day commissioned by Jesus.

Gathered together with Jesus and his disciples in Caesarea Philippi, Peter received the shock of confirmation that Jesus was the Son of God, the true Messiah. In those days, Israel was expecting a hero, an emancipator from God, someone with the ministry of Moses who could deliver them from Rome. Already by those times, some others had considered themselves the Messiah or were recognized by a group of followers as such.[16]

In the following Bible passage, we read that Peter received this vital revelation from the heavenly Father when Jesus asked his disciples, "Who do people say that the Son of Man is?"

Simon Peter answered, "You are the Messiah, the Son of the living God." And Jesus answered him, "Blessed are you, Simon Bar Jonah, for flesh and blood has not revealed this to you, but my Father who is in heaven. I also tell you that you are Peter, and on this Rock, I will build my church, and the gates of hell will not prevail against it. I will give to you the keys of the Kingdom of Heaven, and whatever you bind on earth will be bound in heaven, and whatever you loose on earth will be loosed in heaven." (Matthew 16:16–19 NHEB)

However, the commission given to Peter had a breadth that he could not even imagine. Peter used the "keys" to open the entrance of the Kingdom of Heaven also to the Gentiles! Cornelius and his guests were the first Gentiles (non-Jews) to believe the Gospel.[17] Cornelius, a Roman centurion, was a pious man who believed and feared the God of Israel. In chapter 10 of the book of Acts, we find a very intense but beautiful account of how the first Gentile believers became members of the Church founded by Jesus. Although we do not know precisely how many years passed between the events narrated in chapters 2 and 10, it is estimated that the conversion of the first Gentiles occurred between six and eight years after the birth of the Church. Let us see how it happens as recorded in Acts 10 (NHEB):

Acts 10:1–7: The vision of Cornelius.

Now there was a certain man in Caesarea, Cornelius by name, a centurion of what was called the Italian Regiment, a devout man, and one who feared God with all his house, who gave gifts for the needy generously to the people, and always prayed to God. At about the ninth hour of the day, he saw in a vision an angel of God coming to him, and saying to him, "Cornelius." He, fastening his eyes on him, and being frightened, said, "What is it, Lord?" He said to him, "Your prayers and your gifts to the needy have gone up for a memorial before God. Now send men to Joppa, and get Simon, who is surnamed Peter. He lodges with one Simon, a tanner, whose house is by the seaside." When the angel who spoke to him had departed, he called two of his household servants and a devout soldier of those who waited on him continually. Having explained everything to them, he sent them to Joppa.

Acts 10:9–17: The vision of Peter.

Now on the next day as they were on their journey, and got close to the city, Peter went up on the housetop to pray at about noon. He became hungry and desired to eat, but while they were preparing, he fell into a trance. He saw heaven opened and a certain container descending to him, like a great sheet let down by four corners on the earth, in which were all kinds of four-footed animals of the earth, crawling creatures and birds of the sky. A voice came to him, "Rise, Peter, kill and eat." But Peter said, "Not so, Lord; for I have never eaten anything that is common or unclean." A voice came to him again the second time, "What God has cleansed, you must not call unclean." This was done three times, and immediately the vessel was received up into heaven. Now while Peter was very perplexed within himself what the vision which he had seen might mean, look, the men who were sent by Cornelius, having made inquiry for Simon's house, stood before the gate.

The arrival of the Gentile emissaries with their accounts of the angelic apparition illuminates Peter's vision. In essence, Peter must be prepared first to admit Gentiles into the nascent Church since these were considered impure like the animals of his vision.

Then, Peter finally arrived and entered the house of Cornelius. Behaving in a very Jewish -to-Gentile relationship, this is what Peter said: "He [Peter] said to them [The Gentiles in Cornelius house], 'You yourselves know how it is an unlawful thing for a man who is a Jew to join himself or come to one of another nation, but God has shown me that I shouldn't call any man unholy or unclean'" (Acts 10:28 WEB).

The Bible tells us what happened next with regard to the first Gentiles; conversion:

> While Peter was still speaking these words, the Holy Spirit fell on all those who heard the word. They of the circumcision who believed were amazed, as many as came with Peter, because the gift of the Holy Spirit was also poured out on the Gentiles. For they heard them speaking in other tongues and magnifying God. Then Peter answered, "Can anyone withhold the water, that these who have received the Holy Spirit as well as we, should not be baptized?" He commanded them to be baptized in the name of Jesus Christ. Then they asked him to stay some days. (Acts 10:44–48 WEB)

Let us note that the two human groups the Bible deals with, Jews and Gentiles,[18] now have the same access to the Kingdom of Heaven. This had been God's plan from the beginning, all through the seed of Abraham and David, and punctually executed by the apostle Peter when he was commissioned by Jesus. Furthermore, note the miraculous intervention of the Holy Spirit, empowering the Jewish believers and breaking centuries of separation between Jews and Genties.

Nowhere in the Christian scriptures is Peter found to have written that Jesus established him as the foundation of the Church. On the contrary, the apostle always emphasized in his writings, as did the other inspired writers of the New Covenant, that the Rock of the foundation was Jesus Himself. Therefore, we must understand that the Church has not been founded on any fallible and mortal man but on He who rose from the dead never to die again. [19]

The statement is this:

God commissioned the Jewish people to reach the Gentiles for His Church, not the other way around. The Jewish Bible is full of predictions about the entrance of non-Jews into the kingdom of the God of Abraham, Isaac, and Jacob. This fulfills God's promise to Abraham that all the earth's families will be blessed through His Seed (Genesis 12:1-3).

STATEMENT 5: THE CHRIST OF THE GENTILE CHURCH IS NO OTHER THAN THE JEWISH MESSIAH.

The meaning of *Christ*, from which the words *Christian* and *Christianity* [20] are derived, comes from the Greek translation of the Hebrew title and concept Messiah. It, therefore, means something that is also very Jewish. Throughout his Gospel, John stressed that both words, *Christ* and *Messiah*, refer to the same one, the

Alfredo Calderon-Rodriguez

Jewish Messiah. *There is no such thing as a Messiah created by and for the Gentiles*; there is only a real one, the one John dealt with in his writings. John made sure to make this extremely clear: "He first finds his brother Simon, and saith unto him, we have found the Messiah, which is, being interpreted, the Christ" (John 1:41 KJV). "The woman said to him, 'I know that Messiah comes, he who is called Christ. When he has come, he will declare to us all things.' Jesus said to her, 'I am he, the one who speaks to you'" (John 4:25–26 WEB).

As I mentioned before in Statement 4, the first Jesus responders were all Jewish and followed their Jewish Messiah. In other words, Jesus was so Jewish that His followers of the circumcision believed they would continue with this separation. So, it is not a surprise that, after so many centuries of partition between Jews and Gentiles, there would be resistance on the Jewish followers of Jesus to accept Gentiles in the nascent Church.

Even in Jesus's ascension to heaven, registered in Acts chapter 1, we can understand how Jewish those first Jesus followers were:

> Therefore, when they had come together, they asked him, "Lord, are you now restoring the kingdom to Israel?" He said to them, "It is not for you to know times or seasons which the Father has set within his own authority. But you will receive power when the Holy Spirit has come upon you. You will be my witnesses in Jerusalem, in all Judea and Samaria, and to the farthest part of the earth. (Acts 1:6–8 NHEB)

Look at the question they asked in such a dramatic moment as this! It not only reflects the Jewish-messianic conception of the figure of Jesus among all His followers, but it also reflects the Jewish-messianic endowment of Jesus!

You are the Messiah!

What happened in Cornelius's house, and how difficult it became for Peter to overcome himself, continued to occur in other instances. Right after Peter came back to Jerusalem from Cornelius's house, he was called by the Jewish believers and Church leaders to request an explanation.

> Now the apostles and the brothers who were in Judea heard that the Gentiles had also received the word of God. When Peter had come up to Jerusalem, those who were of the circumcision contended with him, saying, "You went into uncircumcised men, and ate with them!" (Acts 11:1–3 WEB)

> If then God gave to them the same gift as to us, when we believed in the Lord Jesus Christ, who was I, that I could withstand God?" When they heard these things, they held their peace, and glorified God, saying, "Then God has also granted to the Gentiles repentance to life!" (Acts 17–18 WEB)

The jealousy of the Jewish believers about the Good News of Jesus made them very careful in handling these issues. Old experiences narrated in the Jewish Bible [21] about the consequences of disobeying God in joining with Gentiles had made them act in a very safe way. Chapter 15 of the book of Acts gives us an excellent example of this clash of feelings.

It takes the diligence and compromise of another Jewish believer, the Apostle Paul (Shaul), to keep "the gates open" for the Gentiles. In that way, he became known as the Apostle of the Gentiles. [22] But despite his intense dedication to preaching the Gospel to the Gentiles, Paul never ceased to love his people of Israel with the same passion. These are the words of Paul registered in his letter to the Church in Rome.

> I tell the truth in Christ. I am not lying, my conscience testifying with me in the Holy Spirit that I have great sorrow and unceasing pain in my heart. For I could wish that I myself were accursed from Christ for my brothers' sake, my relatives according to the flesh who are Israelites; whose is the

adoption, the glory, the covenants, the giving of the law, the service, and the promises; of whom are the fathers, and from whom is Christ as concerning the flesh, who is over all, God, blessed forever. Amen. (Romans 9:1–5 WEB)

Jesus, the anointed one, is the physical descent of Paul's nation ancestors! What a declaration! As we can read in this Bible passage, the credit for our faith is related to the roots of Judaism. These roots, substantially described by Paul, nourish the faith that we Christians have in a Jewish savior. Verse 4 says, "to them belong." We can also add the prophets of Israel to this list, the ones Christians believed in, read about, and paid attention to as equal.

The following is another strong declaration of Paul as registered in Romans. I'll let the scripture speak for itself:

> I ask then, did they (Israel) stumble that they might fall? May it never be! But by their fall salvation has come to the Gentiles, to provoke them to jealousy. Now if their fall is the riches of the world, and their loss the riches of the Gentiles, how much more their fullness? For I speak to you who are Gentiles. Since then as I am an apostle to Gentiles, I glorify my ministry; if by any means I may provoke to jealousy those who are my flesh and may save some of them. For if the rejection of them is the reconciling of the world, what would their acceptance be, but life from the dead? If the first fruit is holy, so is the lump. If the root is holy, so are the branches. But if some of the branches were broken off, and you (Gentiles Believers), being a wild olive, were grafted in among them and became partaker with them of the root and of the richness of the olive tree, don't boast over the branches (Israel). But if you boast, it is not

you who support the root, but the root supports
you. You will say then, "Branches were broken off,
that I might be grafted in. True; by their unbelief
they were broken off, and you stand by your faith.
Don't be conceited, but fear; for if God didn't spare
the natural branches, neither will he spare you.
(Romans 11:11–21 WB)

Paul ceased to be a ruthless persecutor of the Church after
personal experience with the risen Jesus. Later, he became an
example of dedication to the cause of the Messiah. Read the story
of his transformation in chapter 9 of Acts.

The statement is this:

**Jesus's Jewish messianism is evident in his
disciples' concept of Him. Jesus always
identified himself as the Messiah, the
one who would come from the House of
Judah. The Christian Bible never denies
that important fact. The Christian Messiah
is no other that the Jewish Messiah.**

STATEMENT 6: ISRAEL HAS NOT BEEN REPLACED BY THE CHRISTIAN CHURCH.

In some Christian circles, there is the belief that the Church has
replaced Israel as God's sole nation on earth. Once the Church
emerged, Israel ended its position as God's nation. This way of
thinking among some Christian circles is known as replacement

theology. But what does the Christian Bible say about this theology? After all, its proposers are based on the same source as others who do not consider it correct.

Replacement theology apparently began as soon as the earthly Church gradually slipped from its Jewish roots. To understand this better, we need to discuss what the Christian Bible says about the Church and its historical manifestation on earth. We must look at how the Church has historically affected the world's nations throughout its existence. Equally, we must look at the impact it has had on the Hebrew nation both in the time of Jesus and during the diaspora. In the second section of this book, we will discuss this in detail.

It is also essential that recognizing the Jewish roots of the Christian faith does not mean that we, as believers and followers of Jesus, have to return to the rituals and liturgy of the Law of Moses. It is more related to the belief in the Jewish Messiah, the One who can save us. The complete chapter 15 of Acts clearly deals with this issue. The entire letter to the Galatians and the letter to the Hebrews clarifies this possible conflict.

Although not all Christian sectors support it, let's analyze replacement theology. Let's explore this topic only in its fundamental belief that the Church has *replaced* Israel as the Nation of God on earth and that, now, the Church is the Israel nation of God, even from the first day of its birth on that celebration of Pentecost nearly two thousand years ago. We must understand also that there may be internal variations among those who support this belief.

Fortunately, as I have mentioned before, we are faced with difficult questions but with straightforward answers from the Bible. Jesus is the best example of this. When a group of religious people came to Him with a woman caught in adultery,[23] they wanted to confront Him with what the Law of Moses dictated in this case. What Jesus did surprise everyone; He did not begin a complicated theology discussion. He confronted them with their wicked intentions. The result: everybody left, and the woman they wanted to stone stayed face to face with someone who could help her and not condemn her. Jesus went properly to the real meaning of the Law of Moses, sanctification, and justice for everyone.

In Matthew 23:1–3, we read: "Then Jesus spoke to the multitude and to his disciples, saying, "The scribes and the Pharisees sit in Moses' seat. Therefore, whatever they tell you to observe, observe and do, but do not do their works; for they say and do not do" (WEB). Jesus was making it clear that sometimes the heartfelt intentions of the religious leaders were not in accord with the justice and compassion contained in the religious system they claimed to minister.

When spies tried to tangle Jesus with matters of the Law of Moses, they asked Him if it was lawful to pay the taxes to Caesar.[24] The simple answer Jesus gave left them unarmed and amazed. He asked them for a Roman coin with the image and inscription of Caesar. Jesus then asked them whose image it was. Upon receiving the correct answer, "'It is Caesar's,' He answered them, 'Render to Caesar the things that are Caesar's, and to God the things that are God's'" (Mark 12:16–17 WEB). They simply left, totally without further words!

By this, I do not mean to say that Christians or other people who believe in replacement theology have deviated hearts. No, please, never. It is just a way of interpreting the Bible that some are inclined to do. I am saying that there should be simple findings in the Christian Bible that enable us to understand this better, and these last two events in which Jesus handled those who confronted him are samples of that.

Human beings always need to know the times that lie ahead. Christian circles are not an exception. Armed with the scriptures, Christian theologians and eschatologists have tried to explain the events to come, creating different opinions about what the Bible says related to the final times.

What will happen to the Church and Israel in the future? What is Israel's relationship with the Church since the Church came into being? These questions have sparked a debate because of the different opinions. Some believe that Israel as a nation is already finished in its role as an instrument of God; it is no more than any other of the nations of the earth. At the opposite extreme, some think that Israel as a nation will, until the return of Jesus, retain its identity as God's nation despite its coexistence with the Church.

Many search the Bible for interpretations of this relationship through the ages. As mentioned before, for some, this issue was defined when the Church took over the baton from Israel. For others, national Israel remains in God's future plans despite its current state of disobedience.

Possibly having a clearer understanding of past events may help us understand our present and future better. In other instances, trying to establish future facts occasionally leads to forced interpretations of some Bible passages.

Although the purpose of this work is not to analyze the different theological currents in Christianity, inevitably and unintentionally, discussing replacement theology has led us to do so in part. With this established, let's move to the core.

The following Bible passage records a historical event registered by Matthew[25] (also expressed in Luke 13:31–35). It may effortlessly help us to understand this issue better. Let us see how Jesus grieved over Jerusalem:

> Jerusalem, Jerusalem, who kills the prophets, and stones those who are sent to her. How often I would have gathered your children together, even as a hen gathers her chicks under her wings, and you would not. Look, your house is left to you desolate. For I tell you, you will not see me from now on, until you say, 'Blessed is he who comes in the name of the Lord.' (Matthew 23:37–39 NHEB)

There are many other relevant passages in the New Testament, but this passage may be enough to erase replacement theology. This passage narrates a historical moment in which Jesus, a few days before He was crucified, was in Jerusalem talking to the people and the religious officials. Let's pay attention to what He said to them:

"For I tell you this, you will not see me from now on, until you say, 'Blessed is he who comes in the name of the Lord!'" (Mathew 2:39 NHEB) To whom was Jesus delivering this prophecy? To whom does Jesus refer when He says, "For I tell you …"? It was to Jerusalem because Jerusalem was and is the eternal spiritual heart of the Jewish nation. Even more, was not to the religious leaders that Jesus tells, "until you say, 'Blessed is he who comes in the name of the Lord'"?

Please take note that, in this historical moment, Jesus was not talking to the Church! In other words, Jesus was not saying this to the Church; he was saying it to the Jewish spiritual heart!

Where was the Church then? It wasn't born yet; it did not exist when Jesus spoke these words. There was a time gap from this event to when the Church was born on the following Pentecost day. The Church came to be some fifty-three to fifty-four days after this event. We cannot be specific about the particular day of Jesus's last week when He confronted the religious leaders with these words, but certainly it has to be in a time frame between three to four days before His crucifixion. (According to Matthew this event happens the second day of Jesus visiting Jerusalem in His last week of ministry. See Matthew 23:29–37.)

In that time gap, these events were to happen: three to four days to Jesus's crucifixion; three more days to the resurrection; the forty days He was appearing to the apostles, disciples, and other witnesses[26]; and seven days of waiting time for the disciples in the upper room. In total, fifty-three to fifty-four days to the day the Church came to be.

So, who are the ones who would receive Jesus with shouts of welcome? Who would be the ones who would shout to him, For I tell you, you will not see me from now on, until you say, 'Blessed is he who comes in the name of the Lord!'" (Mathew 23:39 WEB). Perhaps the day before, Jesus was received in Jerusalem with those same welcoming shouts of messianic celebration by the people of Jerusalem, so this event foretold by Jesus was still in the future. If there not will be a national Israel with Jerusalem as its capital to welcome Jesus with these messianic songs, then who?

At least this Bible passage states very clearly that, by the time of Jesus's second coming, there will be a nation inhabiting Jerusalem. The people will have enough information to expect a Messiah from the heavens. Can it be the Church that has substitute Israel according to this replacement theology? Will a physical church-nation-state be living in Jerusalem at that hour to welcome Jesus for the second time? Or could it be a national Israel with a renewed hope in the promised Messiah?

Trying to see into the future is a challenging task, but surely, -we know that the future is based on the present. The present is always the platform from which the future launches. Guess what? *There is a nation right now living in a country named Israel. It has a capital city named Jerusalem, and they call themselves Israel.*

Not only that, but it is also a nation that affirms and claims by various means to be the genuine descendants of the ancient Jewish nation. It is a nation that, for now, internally has different meanings and notions about the expected Messiah, but on that day predicted by Jesus, will be receiving Him in all His splendor. This fills with hope and joy the hearts of those of us who long for the return of the Messiah! The stage is set!

I was sent only to the lost sheep of the house of

ISRAEL

The people of the Jewish nation were spread throughout all Gentile nations for almost two thousand years. But no matter where they were, they kept their customs, traditions, and the hope (now realized) of returning to the land of their ancestors. Also, alongside the diaspora, there were always Jewish communities living in that portion of disputed territory under the rules of past empires.

Since the rebirth of the State of Israel, the people born after the first immigrants called themselves Sabras or Israelis. This new generation of Israelis are the descendants of those first Jewish immigrants who made Aliyah from the diaspora after two thousand years of exile. Therefore, it is appropriate to identify them as part of the reborn Jewish nation. What are the chances that this fact is valid? Well, there are only two alternatives: To be the true descendants or not.

Let's suppose that the modern state of Israel is one of impersonators. Which is their real identity? How could different impostors from all over the world come together to create a false identity and invade a land that never belonged to them? And not to only invade, but also fight for it, spilling their blood while exposing their families to the horrors of war. What genius or geniuses could organize a fraud so monumental and beyond expectations?

The other only possibility is that they are the real descendants, those whose ancestors once were dispersed and persecuted, people who never gave up hope of returning to their homeland despite a long exile of two thousand years. This nation preserved in keeping its most sacred values, thus joining by an invisible bond so strong, that it turned a valley of dry bones into a vibrant society full of life!

Will this happy welcoming prophesied by Jesus be the moment when Israel will recognize the One we have pierced as Messiah? Let us see what the apostle Paul has to say about what he calls a mystery.

> For I do not desire you to be ignorant, brothers, of this mystery, so that you won't be wise in your own conceits, that a partial hardening has happened to Israel, until the fullness of the Gentiles has come in, and so all Israel will be saved. Even as it is written, "There will come out of Zion the Deliverer, and he will turn away ungodliness from Jacob. This is my covenant to them when I will take away their sins." Concerning the Good News, they are enemies for your sake. But concerning the election, they are loved for the fathers' sake. (Romans 11:25–28 NHEB)

The moment when all Israel will be saved will happen when a single event occurs: When the number of Gentiles who will be saved is completed. Paul called this event a mystery. According to this passage, all of Israel will be saved in its fulfillment (Romans 11:25-28). But how is it going to happen? Will this be when Israel and the Gentile believers in the Jewish Messiah will finally merge into one? If so, when, and how will this mystery be uncovered?

Right now, I cannot answer any of these questions. I believe that that has not yet happened in our present time, April 2023. We can only imagine what these events described by Paul will be like, but for now, it is difficult to predict.

We can also ask ourselves why the apostle Paul, as the apostle of the Gentiles, kept on mentioning the Church and Israel as two different nations in his letter to the Church in Rome. Why, in any other of his apostolic letters, did the apostle Paul never mention that one had replaced the other?

In any case, God could have substituted Israel for another nation of his creation, as he proposed centuries ago when the Hebrew nation provoked Him to wrath for their idolatry on the slopes of Mount Sinai. Why did God honor Moses's intersessions when he advocated for Israel, and did not consume them in his righteous wrath? It makes no sense that God promised Moses not to destroy them, only to replace them in the future with the Church (Exodus 32:9–14).

The apostle Paul did not speak of one replacing the other; it was about two becoming one. On the contrary, he continually described the Church and the Jewish nation as two distinct entities, which at one time were separate. But he also taught that the wall that separated them was broken down by the sacrifice of Jesus to make the two into one people (Ephesians 2:13–16). Two different nations, through Jesus, became one.

The statement is this:

The fact that one nation replaces another means that only one will prevail while the other disappears. The fact that two nations merge in one means that neither will expire; instead, they will complement each other to become one—one eternal nation of God!

When will this union be completed? For now, we are on the threshold of an unfinished operation, an operation of fusion that began at the cross. When Paul wrote to the Ephesians in verses

2:14–16, his message that God had made the two (Israel and the Church) one nation had not yet happened; neither has it happened today. Likewise, in the present tense (verse 6 of chapter 2), Paul expressed that God had resurrected and seated believers in the heavenly realms with Christ. This, too, had not happened either when he wrote it and has not happened in our present time. Paul has considered both statements facts that, without any shadow of a doubt, must take place. Yes, countless Jewish believers in Jesus are part of the universal Church of the Messiah, which is already discussed in this book, but not a national Israel becoming one with the Church.

As everybody may agree, every process takes time to be completed. Should we be immersed in that process right know? That's what the Bible suggests. Only under the love of God who united them as one people will it be possible. God Himself, through His Messiah, made this fusion possible.

After all, the first Hebrew who ever existed was a Gentile; his name was Father Abraham. Before that there were not "us and them." There were not Hebrews and Gentiles. Also, there is only one human race, the human species.

The purpose of God is to recover His most precious treasure, which is humanity. His plan is to make that rescue possible through His Messiah, the Son of God, the Son of David, the Son of Man.

Replacement Theology Reflections

As I have mentioned, replacement theology argues that God finished dealing with Israel as His earthly nation when a New Covenant showed up. As a result, it supports that the present state of Israel, which officially resurfaced among nations on 14 May 1948, is nothing more than a creation of the United Nations or a political impulse of what is often called Zionism. Moreover, God no longer has specific plans for Israel as a nation, either since 1948 or in the future. In other words, presently, in this doctrine standpoint, the modern state of Israel is like any other Gentile (*goy* in Hebrew and Yiddish) nation. In my opinion, this is the most harmful part of this doctrine. Let us see.

Replacement theology has created a kind of justification for Israel detractors in some Christian circles. To see modern Israel as cruel invaders, a false nation, impostors, etc. is one of the results. Another is to look at the modern state of Israel with curiosity, just as a place to travel and see the archaeological remains of an "extinct" nation, the area where the Christian faith was born and from there gradually reached all the nations of the earth. Let us take a closer look at this replacement point of view.

To call the modern state of Israel invaders and false impostors, whether denying their historical connection to their ancestors' land or not, *is a way to delegitimize, in biblical and political terms, their right to a national return*, especially when the most reliable historical data shows that, since the exile provoked by the Roman Empire a century after Jesus's crucifixion, another political state has never existed in that geographical area. That means two thousand years of total absence of a human group that is declared as a state or a country (in its full definition) in that particular spot on the planet.

In that long period, different cultural human groups lived in the area. Those, in a very natural and understandable reaction, tried to fill up the vacuum left by the many empires that had controlled the region over the centuries, most of them not existing anymore. Romans, Byzantines, Mamelukes, Crusaders, Ottomans, British, and the United Nations had controlled the region before the reestablishment of the state of Israel in 1948.

Several human groups, ancient and modern, have also established strong communities in the region. Some have already disappeared or diminished, but others have continued to manifest their presence. Today, there is a large population of Arabs known as Palestinians and a sizeable population of Druze. The Palestinians claim the right to own the land and to start a state of their own. Meanwhile the

Druze community, as for now, lives in peace with a culture of "state within a state."

Also, the Arab and Jewish populations of the city of Jerusalem, the capital of Israel, have been in challenging disputes over claims to their right to possess the city as their capital. But again, precise historical data shows that, in all those two thousand years of exile of the Jewish people, no human group has ever been there as a state or recognized Jerusalem as their capital city.

Expansionism, a solid and natural human behavior, has created an extremely complicated political situation in this region, which is expanded when human rights are jeopardized. Does Israel have the biblical right to return to the land of their ancestors? For this, as discussed before in this chapter, we need to understand at least what the Christian Bible says about all these complex situations.

We can also consider the possibility that, in some replacement theology Christian circles, people may think that the actual state of Israel is truly comprised of the descendants of the ancient Jewish nation—people who, from the exile, for centuries always wondered about returning to the beloved land of their ancestors and who could achieve it after almost two thousand years. This human group is comprised of the people who managed to do so, not within a plan of a divine redemption for a national Israel, but in a purely humanistic, political, and cultural movement. If this is true, then did God allow the Jewish people to return to the land of their ancestors only to protect them from extinction, just for mercy but without any further national redemption purposes? If that is a yes, then why did God not provide the same for other nations that have disappeared from the earth?

But what if God has some unfinished business with Israel, some promises not fulfilled as of now? Is this why God allowed them to return after two thousand years of exile? If we can answer both questions in the affirmative, then the possibility is that God opened the door for this to happen with one even more perfect purpose: *getting humankind ready for the return of the Messiah!*

STATEMENT 7: THE NEW COVENANT WAS MADE WITH THE HOUSE OF ISRAEL.

God did not establish the New Covenant throughout any particular house among the Gentiles. Instead, it was the opposite; it was produced for all humankind through the Jewish people. Then, from there, it was to be given to all humanity.

In a letter to the Hebrews, a book that is part of the Christian Bible, the author quotes the prophet Jeremiah in his pointing to a New Covenant that God would establish with the house of Israel. The reason for a New Covenant that has to be established is that Israel or anyone else had not been able to fulfill the first one, not because the Old Covenant was imperfect, but because no man could meet his high demands (Romans 8:3,7).

Moshe Ben Maimon, one of the most popular and respected extra-biblical figures in Judaism throughout its history, expressed his faith in a coming Messiah. His thirteen principles of faith are today an almost undisputed standard in the Jewish religious sector. Information on these thirteen principles of faith is abundant and readily available, as various Jewish communities comment on them through their websites. There is also abundant literature on the subject. In the twelfth principle it establishes the reality of a Messiah to be expected since he will come without fail.

But why? Why do we wait for a Messiah if God has given humankind the perfect law through Moses? The Creator also gave the holy scriptures to help us reach the goal of redemption. Furthermore, God made a covenant with us humans through the nation of Israel. Will it be necessary for a Messiah to come and execute God's plan flawlessly? Is it because He is the one who comes on behalf of the Lord to save us all? *Is this because God will establish the New Covenant through this Anointed One?*

Both Christians and Jews agree that the requirements of the Law of Moses are so high that no human can carry them out entirely.

That is why there was a need for daily animal sacrifices—to cover up the constant failures. But ironically, this same human weakness is probably the most worrying factor for those honest hearts who really want to serve God.

Questions like the following may awaken in the heart of someone who honestly wants to serve God: Am I following the right leader? Am I on the right path? Am I doing the things required by God correctly? Am I able to satisfy the high demands of the original Covenant expressed through the Law of Moses?

Are our genuine and honest answers to these questions, no? Then we can understand that we need urgent help from someone who loves us enough to offer Himself to satisfy God's just wrath, to receive our deserved punishment in his humanity, and thus save us. *A Messiah cannot redeem humankind without first cleansing its sins! That is what redemption through the Anointed One is all about! That is why the Messiah first needs to purge human debt in Himself and, once the debt is covered in full, be able to redeem it.*

Maybe this is why there are so many different ideas about this Anointed One, even in Judaism. Did each honest self-attempt to figure out a formula for achieving the Law end in failure? Did each failure lead to a continual cover-up action? Did this happen again and again in a never-ending story? Is that why we inadvertently keep making continuous and various sacrifices in our different beliefs? Of course, today we do not make sacrifices the way they were offered in the temple; we do it in different symbolic manners.

Is this human behavior with regard to making sacrifices driven by a guilty conscience that is the result of human incapacities to fulfill God's standards, which are written in every human soul as the Bible says in Romans 2:14–16? Is this a universal conduct, an effort to calm an accusatory conscience? Is this the reason there have been uncountable different religions and cults throughout human history? Is this why even science is a kind of religion for some "non-religious" people? But the most crucial question should be this: Is this Messiah capable of helping us to have a better conscience to stand before God? Let's see what the book of Hebrews says about a clean conscience before God: "How much more shall the blood of Christ, who through the eternal Spirit offered himself without blemish unto God, cleanse your conscience from dead works to serve the living God?" (Hebrew 9:14 WEB).

After all, the divine demand in the First Covenant required us to be perfect before God, which is entirely understandable because the God with whom we commit ourselves to a covenant is perfect, so should we be.

If perfect religion is the fulfillment of a set of rules given by God, then, for those who believe that the Bible is the inspired Word of God, we must understand that we must follow all that God requires in the Bible. The question is: can we?

Again, the problem is that these standards are beyond the reach of any human being. The only way we can be with God for eternity is to be like Him. In this way, we can understand that we need someone who can do it, is capable, commissioned, and empowered by God, somebody who, out of love, enforces it as if we had done it. This is the perfect picture of a lamb to be slaughtered. Because the price for our sin needs to be covered but covered with innocent blood, as pointed out in the First Covenant.

Therefore, this Anointed One, the One who comes in the name of the Lord, may fulfill that Old Covenant, *and finish the continuous sacrifices. Hosanna* means "save now" or "save please," and this will be the shout of joy for welcoming the Messiah. Curiously, Jesus once was received with those shouts in Jerusalem as we mentioned in the preceding chapter. In the next theme to discuss, there will be more on that (Matthew 21:8–11, Mark 11:1–11, Luke 19:29–40, John 12:12–19).

Let us look at the words of Jesus concerning the New Covenant:

> The day of unleavened bread came on which the
> Passover lamb must be sacrificed. Jesus sent *Peter and*

John, saying, "Go and prepare the Passover for us, that we may eat." (Luke 22:7-8 WEB, emphasis mine).

When the hour had come, he sat down with the twelve apostles. He said to them, "I have earnestly desired to eat this Passover with you before I suffer, for I tell you, I will no longer by any means eat of it until it is fulfilled in God's Kingdom." He received a cup, and when he had given thanks, he said, "Take this, and share it among yourselves, for I tell you, I will not drink at all again from the fruit of the vine, until God's Kingdom comes." He took bread, and when he had given thanks, he broke, and gave it to them, saying, "This is my body which is given for you. Do this in memory of me." Likewise, he took the cup after supper, saying, *"This cup is the New Covenant in my blood, which is poured out for you.* (Luke 22:14–20 WEB, emphasis mine)

Why during Passover? Jesus was establishing the New Covenant in His sacrifice. His body and blood were to be the Lamb of Pesah, the Lamb of God, the Lamb of deliverance. Who in the history of humanity has ever done or said anything like this? Simply no one but Jesus!

This celebration is an event related to the revelation of God in the Jewish scriptures. Look at how Jewish all this was—a Jewish rabbi, a Jewish festival, all Jewish disciples, and Jewish significance! Where were the customs and culture of the Gentiles in this event? Simply nowhere.

Alfredo Calderon-Rodriguez

I will make a New Covenant with the House of Israel

and with the House of Judah

This New Covenant was made for the House of Israel, and we, the Gentiles, were grafted in; we were not left out.

The Christian Bible links this New Covenant to its origin in the Jewish scriptures. The author of the Epistle to the Hebrews quotes and interprets what the prophet Jeremiah wrote in chapter 31, verses 31-34 of the book that bears his name.

> For finding fault with them, he said, "Behold, the days come", says the Lord, "that I will make a new covenant with the house of Israel and with the house

of Judah; not according to the covenant that I made with their fathers, in the day that I took them by the hand to lead them out of the land of Egypt; for they didn't continue in my covenant, and I disregarded them," says the Lord. "For this is the covenant that I will make with the house of Israel. After those days," says the Lord; "I will put my laws into their minds, I will also write them on their heart. I will be their God, and they will be my people. They will not teach every man his fellow citizen, and every man his brother, saying, 'Know the Lord,' for all will know me, from their least to their greatest. For I will be merciful to their unrighteousness. I will remember their sins and lawless deeds no more. (Hebrews 8:8–12 WEB)

What laws was Prophet Jeremiah referring to? Specifically, the one that was going to be in people's minds and hearts. Well, the word *law* traduced from the original Greek is *Nomos*, and the translation from the Hebrew to Greek is *Torah*! Let's see Jeremiah message again as mentioned by the author of the Epistle to the Hebrews in the text mentioned above: *"I will put my laws into their minds, I will also write them on their heart"*. Probably this means something more than tying leather boxes containing scriptures onto the arms and forehead, even though this is a genuine human effort to please God. What this probably means is that the perfect justice of the Law, eventually, will be part of our inner nature, something that we not just practice, but live!

How does Jesus describe this new approach to the Law of Moses? Let's see:

The fulfillment of the law:

"Don't think that I came to destroy the law or the prophets. I didn't come to destroy, but to fulfill.

For most certainly, I tell you, until heaven and earth pass away, not even one smallest letter or one tiny pen stroke shall in any way pass away from the law, until all things are accomplished. Therefore, whoever shall break one of these least commandments and teach others to do so, shall be called least in the Kingdom of Heaven; but whoever shall do and teach them shall be called great in the Kingdom of Heaven. For I tell you that unless your righteousness exceeds that of the scribes and Pharisees, there is no way you will enter into the Kingdom of Heaven. (Matthew 5:17–32 WEB)

Murder:

"You have heard that it was said to the ancient ones, 'You shall not murder; and 'Whoever murders will be in danger of the judgment.' But I tell you that everyone who is angry with his brother without a cause will be in danger of the judgment. Whoever says to his brother, 'Raca!' will be in danger from the council. Whoever says, 'You fool!' will be in danger of the fire of Gehenna." If therefore you are offering your gift at the altar, and there remember that your brother has anything against you, leave your gift there before the altar, and go your way. First be reconciled to your brother, and then come and offer your gift. Agree with your adversary quickly while you are with him on the way; lest perhaps the prosecutor delivers you to the judge, and the judge delivers you to the officer, and you be cast into prison. Most certainly I tell you, you shall by no means get out of there until you have paid the last penny. (Matthew 5:17–26 WEB)

Adultery:

> "You have heard that it was said, 'You shall not commit adultery;' but I tell you that everyone who gazes at a woman to lust after her has committed adultery with her already in his heart. If your right eye causes you to stumble, pluck it out and throw it away from you. For it is more profitable for you that one of your members should perish than for your whole body to be cast into Gehenna. If your right hand causes you to stumble, cut it off, and throw it away from you. For it is more profitable for you that one of your members should perish, than for your whole body to be cast into Gehenna. (Matthew 5:27–30 WEB)

Divorce:

> "It was also said, 'Whoever shall put away his wife, let him give her a writing of divorce, but I tell you that whoever puts away his wife, except for the cause of sexual immorality, makes her an adulteress; and whoever marries her when she is put away commits adultery. (Matthew 5:31–32 WEB)

Strong words from Jesus. This time He was making clear the importance of the Law of Moses (Torah). In Jesus's words, we can find that the real purpose of the Law was not to be a set of rules to be obeyed externally or ritually by every person on earth. On the contrary, it was a power to propel a supernatural process of spiritual transformation in human hearts, a change from a human nature to a spiritual one (John 3:1-16).

We cannot fulfill the perfect Law of Moses because of our fallen human nature. Only the Messiah could meet the Law requirements and, in that way, redeem us from sin through himself. When John the Baptist identified Jesus as the Lamb of God, he meant that He would be our atonement.[27]

The book of Hebrews, especially chapters eight and nine, is a must read, a beautiful narrative of Jesus's sacrifice. As is taught in the book to the Hebrews, Jesus offered His life as the only perfect sacrifice, and because it was perfect, it was made only once. This means no more sacrifices because God's redemption plans were set forever with this perfect one!

That is the work of the Messiah. That is why we need Him; that's why people will call out "Hosanna!" at the full installment of His Kingdom at His return!

Now we can live with the hope of total redemption because we can have the justice of the Law in our new nature; it has replaced the old fallen nature by faith in the Messiah (Romans 8:1–4).

As Prophet Jeremiah established, Paul, too, taught the need for a New Covenant in his letter to the Romans, all because of our human incapability to strictly fulfill the requirements of the original one.

The statement is this:

This New Covenant was made for the House of Israel, and we, the Gentiles, were grafted in! The simplicity of Jesus's teaching abolishes any other way to reach the Kingdom of Heaven away from His person. That is why the Messiah is necessary for a New Covenant! That is why God Himself promoted the Anointed One, the only one who could fulfill the Law given through Moses, the only one who could accomplish the Old Covenant.

Apostle Paul was very emphatic about this particular statement. He wrote to the Gentile Church in Rome: "But if some of the branches were broken off, and you, being a wild olive, were grafted in among them and became partaker with them of the root and of the richness of the olive tree, don't boast over the branches. But if you boast, it is not you who support the root, but the root supports you" (Romans 11:17–18 WEB)

Chapter 11 of the Epistle to the Roman Church in the Christian side of the Bible (Romans 11) it is a must read. It explains many things.

Let us see again Jesus's words about the Old Covenant: "Do not think that I have come *to abolish the Law or the Prophets*; I have not come to abolish them *but to fulfill them*" (Matthew 5:17 WEB, my emphasis)

As I have noted, the New Covenant, the Law of Moses, and the Messiah are inseparable. The Messiah alone has to be the mediator between both pacts and the mediator between God and us!

SECTION 2

THREE ADDITIONAL ISSUES

ISSUE 1: DOUBLE-PACT THEOLOGY

Dual covenant theology is another somewhat confusing interpretation. It states that both covenants are fully operative simultaneously and that the primary human problem will be to choose between them or perhaps to mix them for the sake of convenience. In this interpretation, it is said that Jesus came primarily for the Gentiles, that *the Jewish people count on the Law of Moses for their rescue, and that they do not necessarily need Jesus.* Fortunately, a simple analysis also applies to this theological thinking.

Again, a simple statement by Jesus, even though there is much more information in the Christian Bible about it, destroys this assumption. In the following biblical passage, Jesus states that He was sent only to the lost sheep of Israel. As I have discussed before, we Gentiles were grafted into God's covenants with Israel, not the other way around.

Let us look at the following Bible passage again:

> Jesus went out from there and withdrew into the region of Tyre and Sidon. Behold, a Canaanite woman came out from those borders and cried, saying, "Have mercy on me, Lord, you son of David! My daughter is severely possessed by a demon!" But he answered her not a word. His disciples came and begged him, saying, "Send her away; for she cries after us." But he answered, "I wasn't sent to anyone but the lost sheep of the house of Israel." (Matthew 15:21–24 WEB)

Jesus's words are sometimes difficult to understand; if you keep reading this passage, you will realize that Jesus was amazed by the faith of that Gentile woman. Notice that she called Him Son of David. Isn't that a Jewish Messianic title? Isn't it a great thing that the heart of a Gentile and a despised woman discovered the ministry of Jesus and expressed it with this simple phrase? Jesus honored her faith and worked a miracle in her life because she believed in Him. This is another great example of believing. Jesus probably wanted to give His disciples a real-life lesson to show what all people can expect from Him.

You will not see me again until you say,

"Blessed is He who comes in the name of the Lord".

Many speculations can arise about the double covenant belief. Why then did Jesus come as a Jewish rabbi if He was to be for the Gentiles primarily? As the Son of God, He could easily have come as a Gentile Messiah and, in his teachings, said so. Or, looking at it from the opposite side, what would be more comfortable for a Gentile? Believe in a non-Jewish Messiah or a Jewish one? Besides, who would save the Jews? Another Messiah? One exclusively directed at the Jews?

If you have only the Law of Moses to save you, then is it Moses the Messiah as the bearer of this immensely beautiful and sacred Law given by God? If Moses is the Messiah, why then did he write about someone who was to come, sent by God, and who was not himself? (Deuteronomy 18:14–19, John 5:46–47.)

History has taught us that, as in Judaism, in the Gentile world too, so many false messiahs have shown up from time to time. That has cost the lives of many fanatic followers of those impostors while driving them to failure. Therefore, there is a need for a single anointed messiah of God, and *this must be the Messiah who was foretold in the Old Covenant and described in the New Covenant*. He is the one who comes to save Jews and Gentiles alike.

Let's use another Bible quote, this one from the Apostle Paul in which it is clearly stated that the Gospel is from and for the Jews too:

> For I am not ashamed of the gospel of Christ: for it is the power of God unto salvation to everyone that believeth; to the Jew first, and also to the Greek. [The Greeks here as a representation for all Gentiles]. (Romans 1:16 KJV)

To complete this theme of the double covenant, let us look at the words Jesus said. When Thomas asked Jesus about the way to salvation, the Lord answered him categorically:

> Thomas said to him, "Lord, we don't know where you are going. How can we know the way?" Jesus said to him, "I am the way, the truth, and the life. No one comes to the Father, except through me. (John 14:5–6 WEB)

The issue is this:

If no one can fulfill the perfect Law of Moses, how is it possible that anyone can be saved by doing so? Furthermore, why will a suffering and/or conquering Messiah be necessary if people can attain their salvation by perfectly fulfilling the Law of Moses? Will a suffering Messiah be necessary exclusively for non-Jews and a conquering one for Jews?

How could this Messiah pay the consequences of our sins and deviations in himself? First, He could offer Himself in weakness as our substitute, taking upon Himself the punishment deserved by us, and second, then becoming our champion, having thus conquered the right to our forgiveness. To do so, He must be someone who satisfies the perfect wrath of God.

ISSUE 2: THE VEIL OF MOSES

But why does Judaism not understand the Christian faith if it comes from the Jews? Let's see what the Christian Bible says about it.

In his second epistle to the Corinthians, Paul said something about "the veil of Moses." He referred to the view that exists in Judaism about the Christian Church. This way of seeing

Christianity through the veil of Moses can be understood through four critical concepts.

1- Jesus did not fulfill, in the eyes of the religious leaders, the preconceived concept of the Messiah as a conquering political priest.
2- Earlier and later self-proclaimed or appointed messiah figures failed, sometimes with bloody consequences.
3- The sudden inclusion of Gentiles in what was for centuries only a purely Jewish hope was rejected in conjunction with non-Jewish customs and culture.
4- Over time, syncretism gradually contaminated the original faith, deriving in a nominal and religious Christianity. This led to confused nominal, historical, and cultural Christianity with the spiritual body of Christ. Or, perhaps, to confuse cultures, sometimes they are not even religious, which can lead to considering some nations as "Christian nations."

Institutional, cultural, or religious Christianity is like any other religion on earth except that nominal Christianity has borrowed Jewish scriptures and integrated them into its faith. But Christianity is different when it comes to an individual's personal experience with the living God through the Messiah and the scriptures. For this reason, the Church cannot be an organization or institution that claims to represent Christ in the world exclusively. If it did, it would create significant confusion among those who want to seek God through the Anointed One.

Questions such as the following would arise: Which is the true Church? Which one should I join if I want to find salvation? How can I be sure that the Christian organization of my membership is the right one?

Well, the best answer to these questions is another question: Why has God given his Messiah to save us if we can get salvation by choosing the right institution or religion? In the second section of this book, we will see Jesus giving a Jewish audience a complete description of the nature of the earthly Church.

The fact is that various religious organizations claim to be the only way to God. Some creeds proclaim that you will not reach that divine rescue if you do not belong to them as a member. Others claim that their organization is the Church that Jesus founded, so faithful membership is required. But, if Jesus proclaimed that the only way to the Father is Himself, what does this mean? Well, this simply means that the Messiah is Jesus, a person, and not an institution.[28]

Although the Church of Jesus can and should be structured in different organizations, it also will have various cultural expressions. However, membership in such bodies is not a requirement for salvation. The Bible teaches about the vital importance of regular meetings of the believers, but this is not an additional condition for our salvation. If that were the case, the Messiah offered his life in an incomplete sacrifice because complementary ways are required. If something additional is needed, then He was not the Lamb of God, and His atonement was not perfect in God's eyes. The author of the book of Hebrews, in chapter 10, quotes Psalm 40:6–8 and explains it under the New Covenant light.

There is an excellent example in the Bible of someone who probably never visited a synagogue, was never a member of any religion, and, in fact, never attended a meeting with Jesus and His disciples and was never baptized. This is one of the thieves crucified with the Lord in the same event. He discovered his Savior in the last moments of his life and found eternal salvation by believing in Jesus (Luke 23:32–43).

Anyway, regular meetings of the Church are essential for many reasons—encouragement, mutual edification, knowing each other, sharing knowledge from the scriptures, helping each other in prayer, and many other benefits. The Church is a body of believers who have been acting by faith on this planet throughout time. The most notorious of those times in the last twenty-one centuries. A believer can't live outside the Church body because the Church is where the Lord manifests the most. There is nothing like a group of believers together. There is no better place to be as one in the Spirit of the Lord while worshiping our common and lovely Savior (Psalm 133, Hebrews 10:25). As a cell cannot live outside the organism it belongs to, the believer needs nourishment from the body to grow and reach his or her purpose. To be a follower of Christ was never and is not the business of a Lone Ranger or Lonely Wolf.

Going back to the Veil of Moses, the Apostle Paul wrote the following, almost two thousand years ago:

> For truly that which has been made glorious has not been made glorious in this respect, by reason of the glory that surpasses. For if that which passes away was with glory, much more that which remains is in glory. Having therefore such a hope, we use great boldness of speech, and not as Moses, who put a veil on his face, that the children of Israel would not look steadfastly on the end of that which was passing away. But their minds were hardened, for until this very day at the reading of the old covenant the same veil remains, because in Christ it passes away. But to this day, when Moses is read, a veil lies on their heart. But whenever one turns to the Lord, the veil is taken away. Now the Lord is the Spirit and where the Spirit of the Lord is, there is liberty. But we all, with unveiled face looking as in a mirror the glory of the Lord, are transformed into the same image from glory to glory, even as from the Lord, the Spirit. (2 Corinthians 3:10–18 NHEB)

For to this day

the same
veil remains

We have, then, that this veil of Moses is not the one that separates the holy of holies from the upper chamber (Matthew 27:50–54). Neither is it the veil that Moses used to cover his face when he came down from Sinai. Symbolically it refers to the religious resistance that the Jewish nation has presented to the figure of Jesus as the emerging Messiah, the same Jesus that the apostles first preached to those of their nation. This rejection has been crowned by centuries of additional and continuing rabbinical teachings as we come to the present day.[29]

This objection to the Messianic identity of Jesus was amplified over the centuries by a continual gentilization of the fundamental doctrine of the original New Testament Church. By gentilization, we mean the gradual substitution or addition of Gentile ecclesiastical doctrines to the basic biblical values of the first-century Church. We could mention the sacred and obligated beliefs that have to be attributed to figures, places, customs, cultic ideologies, organizations, persons, and things like that, which have nothing to do with the original teachings inspired by the Holy Spirit and taught by the apostles.

As for the process of transculturation and addition of Gentile cultural expressions and values in the churches that exist worldwide, this is very different from the process of gentilization mentioned in the previous paragraph. The inclusion or contribution of Gentile customs and values that have become part of the Church as the Gospel has spread throughout the world have enriched the Christian cult with their music, languages, architecture, literature, and other particular expressions of the nations reached. This transcultural process does not change the fundamental apostolic doctrine; rather, it adds a new and rich multicultural dimension to the Christian faith. [30]

There is no doubt that the Gospel began with the Jewish people, and the first followers of Christ were all Jews. Moreover, in the early century of Christianity, most of Jesus's followers were Jews. Then, what happened that resulted in most Jews still not believing that Jesus is their Messiah?

If Moses and the Jewish divisions of the scriptures point to him, as Jesus himself told us,[31] why this present disbelief? As we mentioned before, it seems that this is the time of disobedience for Israel, as discussed in Statement 6. Will this time of national Jewish doubt be the period in which the number of Gentiles is being completed? A fascinating subject to fnd!

The issue is this:

One day this veil is going to be removed by God Himself. The Christian Bible assures emphatically that, at a particular time still in the future, all national Israel will be saved (Romans 11:25–27, 2 Corinthians 3:16).

ISSUE 3: THE FAITH OF FATHER ABRAHAM

What is faith? How many different kinds of faith there are? Which is the best or the real faith, if any? Why are there are so many faith expressions among humankind?

The Bible teaches us that there are only two kinds of faith. The first is that which the human heart develops. The second is that which God offers as a gift.

That which develops the human heart is a natural product of humanity's very existence. We can see this exhibited in countless different religious and philosophical expressions within every nation that exists or has ever existed. Human faith is a matter of constant growth because it is acquired from the culture in which each one is born. It is also naturally evolves and it is continuously transmitted as part of the experiences of the peoples of the world.

The need in human nature to be reconnected with the superior realms is so strong that we can even think that there is a distinct religious expression for each person who has ever existed. This is because no one ever interprets life precisely as others do. We can probably define religion as the human effort to please what we perceive as the supreme of all things, which may be one or many deities or the exaltation of the personal or collective human ego.

God gives the other expression of faith as a gift. It focuses on a unique savior figure. No human heart can produce this kind of faith; rather, it is granted by God to everyone who longs for it. It originates in God's heart and derives from His love for humanity. He gave us faith because God's standards are too high for any human to reach, all because He is perfection in its most elevated expression. "God so loved the world that he gave his one and only Son, that whoever *believes in him* shall not perish but have eternal life" (John 3:16 WEB, emphasis mine)

But why does faith and not work? Well, Apostle Paul answered this question: "For it is by grace you have *been saved, through faith—* and this is not from yourselves, it is the gift of God—not by works, so that no one can boast" (Ephesians 2:8–9 WEB, emphasis mine)

It doesn't matter that faith produces activity and works from the believer; those are only the result of the gift from God. This gifted faith is not passive; it is very active in human hearts. It also makes us grow in all senses. John, the apostle, tells us about the spectacular growth that faith provokes in those who treasure it in their hearts (1 John 3:1–3). In that sense, no more buying front seats in temples to receive credit, no more fasting, no more prayers, no more tithing or offering contests, no more ego. It is God and God alone who saves.

All kinds of good things we do are correct when we give God's the credit, the honor, and the power to save. "Humble yourselves in the sight of the Lord, and he will exalt you" (James 4:10 WEB).

The human kind of faith has so many different meanings for the people. But the faith that is given by God is a treasure that has to be protected by the recipient. It's worth fighting for. "That the proof of your faith, which is more precious than gold that perishes even though it is tested by fire, may be found to result in praise, glory, and honor at the revelation of Jesus Christ" (1 Peter 1:7 WEB).

The faith that God has given us is a precious gift that we need to care for and maintain throughout our lives. Paul, moving into his final days, expressed the following: "*I have fought the good fight. I have finished the course. I have kept the faith.* From now on, the crown of righteousness is stored up for me, which the Lord, the righteous judge, will give to me on that day; and not to me only, but also to all those who have loved his appearing" (2 Timothy 4:7–8 WEB, emphasis mine).

As there is much more information about faith in the Bible, let's fix on the author of this kind of faith. Jesus Himself is the creator of that faith, and that faith was given with a purpose; that is, to honor God by believing and trusting in Him. "Looking to *Jesus, the author and perfecter of faith*, who for the joy that was set before him endured the cross, despising its shame, and has sat down at the right hand of the throne of God" (Hebrews 12:2 WEB, emphasis mine).

What more we can say about something for which there are neither enough words nor time to describe. Well, we can add that this given faith does not convert you to a fanatic; rather, you become somebody who trusts in a living God. We can describe it as trusting faithfully in God while waiting, even though the uncomfortable circumstances in front of your eyes seems not to change. We can say also that faith does not change reality but overcomes and surpasses it.

Ask the three young Hebrews in front of the horrible furnace. The furnace never disappeared; instead, it was overheated, but when they went into it, its consuming power was eliminated. The pit was real for Joseph, also the prison in Egypt, but no matter; God's provision was always a reality in his life for a greater purpose.

Let us look at Father Abraham when he was asked to offer the son of the promise in sacrifice. The mountain was there, and all the things required for the sacrifice were prepared; those things never disappear, but in Abraham's heart there was a kind of faith that made him able to overcome those circumstances. "Abraham said to his young men, "Stay here with the donkey. The boy and I will go over there. *We will worship and come back to you*" (Genesis 22:5 WEB, emphasis mine).

By faith Abraham...

Wow! They all were not religious fanatics; they were people who grabbed, protected, appreciated, and cultivated God's gift of faith. There are so many other examples in the Bible!

Chapter 11 of the book Hebrews is a must read. It is known as the faith gallery in some Christian circles.

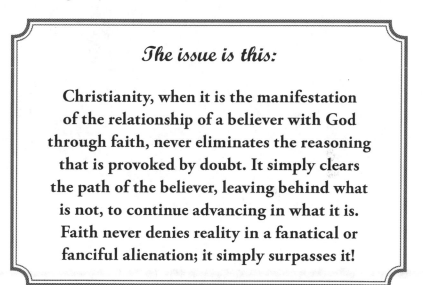

The issue is this:

Christianity, when it is the manifestation of the relationship of a believer with God through faith, never eliminates the reasoning that is provoked by doubt. It simply clears the path of the believer, leaving behind what is not, to continue advancing in what it is. Faith never denies reality in a fanatical or fanciful alienation; it simply surpasses it!

THE HISTORICAL DEVELOPMENT OF THE CHRISTIAN CHURCH AND ITS IMPACT ON THE WORLD: THE EARTHLY CHURCH EXPLAINED IN THE CHRISTIAN BIBLE

THREE CHARACTERISTICS OF THE CHURCH in its earthly stage are very well described by Jesus and by Moses. The nature of the earthly Church would remain indecipherable to the human mind if Jesus had not deciphered it on earth.

1- **Universalism:** The Church is a universal spiritual body in its most pure essence. It's not a human institution ruled by a social-religious hierarchy even though it has leaders, teachers, history, servants, and it's structured. It's more like an organism than an organization.

2- **Dual Personality:** The manifestation of the nominal earthly Church is dual. It is good and evil, true, and false. On the non-kosher side, the worldly Church is composed of a religious mentality of superiority and exclusivity, sometimes expressed in self-righteousness and manipulation, and at other times with violence. Extra-biblical human criteria, personal concepts, so-called revelations of their most influential figures, and historically dragged cultural aspects are imposed, sadly, in the name of the "true and unique faith" (theirs). This mentality is destroyed when we know that the Messiah is not a human institution but the Son of the living God. History has many proofs of horrible things committed by so-called Christian people or Christian institutions, among them cults and mysterious secret organizations that deal with occultism.

The other manifestation of Christianity comes from people who, through their faith in the Messiah, have been redeemed. Regardless of being members of different Christian institutions of all times and places, the experiences of believers and their acceptance of Jesus as their savior are purely personal. These people are convinced through a unique faith and have found deep satisfaction and confirmation in their hearts that they have finally found "the way" for their lives. Believers in Jesus strive to do their best on this path, placing their trust in a Savior they believe in without seeing Him, a Christ who came, died, rose, ascended to heaven, and will soon return, a Savior who is a reality but invisible to our eyes for now. This dual personality of the earthly Church is discussed more in detail ahead.

3- **The Dual Effect:** As for its dual personality, the earthly Church will have a double impact on the Jewish nation: anger, and jealousy. Moses talked about it around fifteen hundred years before the birth of the Church.[32]

CHARACTERISTIC 1: UNIVERSALISM

The Church is a catholic or a universal body, not a specific human institution. To understand this better, we must look at how the Christian Church is described in the Bible. We will find that the Church is composed of people from all times, nations, tribes, and tongues. In order to function more effectively, the human groups that make up the Church have to work in organizations. But despite the necessary institutionalization, the Church goes beyond that categorization. We have to look in the Christian Bible and search for the words of Jesus on this matter. There is no more authoritative figure than Jesus, the reason for the Church to exist.

> But as touching the resurrection of the dead, have ye not read that which was spoken unto you by God, saying, I am the God of Abraham, and the God of Isaac, and the God of Jacob? God is not the God of the dead, but of the living. (Matthew 22:31–32 KJV)

> Jesus answered them, "Isn't this because you are mistaken, not knowing the Scriptures, nor the power of God? For when they will rise from the dead, they neither marry, nor are given in marriage, but are like angels in heaven. But about the dead, that they are raised; haven't you read in the book of Moses, about the Bush, how God spoke to him, saying, 'I am the God of Abraham, the God of Isaac, and the God of Jacob'? (Exodus 3:6) He is not the God of the dead, but of the living. You are therefore badly mistaken." (Mark 12:25–27 WEB)

The Church is the body of believers that has been growing since ancient times. In both Bible passages presented here, the Lord mentioned all those who had sought God from the heart and were not present in their human bodies when Jesus made these statements. He referred to them as living in the presence of God. This is the meaning of universalism. It is interesting to see in the Bible that, immediately after the sin of the fathers of humankind, God quickly dealt with the problem of evil and made them a promise of ransom and redemption (Genesis 3:14–15).

It is simply marvelous that there is a living Church that is in the presence of the Lord constantly. It is a church made up of people who have been forgiven for their sins. These people will never die. They are of all ages and nations. And all of this is through God's gift, His Son. That is the meaning of Jesus's words when he has said, "Now he is not the God of the dead, but of the living, for all are alive to him" (Luke 20:38 WEB).

Some died waiting for Him but believing,[33] others saw him with their own eyes and followed Him.[34] Others believe in Him because of the testimony from those who were close to Him when He came to earth the first time.[35] The common denominator among believers is that they all have received the gift of a transformative faith that has grown in them because it has been valued more than gold.[36] It is this common faith that made the believers a Church made up of Jews and Gentiles.

God did not send His Son to redeem the world through human institutions, even though some of them are founded around the figure of Jesus. God redeemed the world through the vicarious sacrifice of Jesus. The duty of the various churches and institutions that identify themselves as Christian here on earth is to emphasize their Redeemer and not themselves. Their function is to diminish in the manner of John the Baptist while operating the message of the Gospel (John 3:29–30).

A membership card proving membership to any Christian institution doesn't mean we are part of the Church as the body of the Messiah. We are not saved because we belong to a certain Christian organization; we are saved by faith in the Redeemer. We, Christ followers, almost certainly belong to one of the many

Christian institutions, but the closer to the Bible is their message, the better. Jesus, speaking about this, said, "Then two men will be in the field: one will be taken, and one will be left. Two women will be grinding at the mill: one will be taken, and one will be left. Watch therefore, for you don't know in what hour your Lord comes" (Matthew 24:40–42 WEB).

For the Christians, Jesus first came as Ben-Joseph and will return one day as Ben-David. Altogether with Israel, the Church waits also for this Man of God, the anointed one, the Son of God! Interestingly, the last two verses of the Christian part of the Bible says: "He which testified these things saith, surely, I come quickly. Amen. Even so, come, Lord Jesus. The grace of our Lord Jesus Christ be with you all. Amen" (Revelation 22:20-21 KJV).

CHARACTERISTIC 2: DUAL PERSONALITY

In chapter 13 of Matthew, Jesus describes so entirely the worldly Church that there is no doubt about why this dual personality exhibited by the earthly Church shows up. Notice that I call it "earthly Church" or "worldly Church." The earthly Church is the one that humanity can see in its physical presence, can feel its different manifestations, and can interpret throughout its historical and actual existence. This worldly Church manifests itself in various forms. It manifests in its activities, claims, doctrines, projection, and proselytism.

Let's go to Matthew 13; in this chapter are registered various parables of Jesus explaining the nature of His Kingdom on earth, from its beginnings to its final depuration. In these parables, we can see the Church as the anticipation of the full manifestation of God's Kingdom on Earth. It is interesting to see how the apostle Paul regards the members of the Church as ambassadors of the Kingdom of Heaven. If, by ambassadors, we can understand that the kingdom they represent is yet to come. In this way, we can say that the Church is an embassy[37] on earth of the Kingdom of Heaven; each one of its members is an ambassador. (2 Corinthians 5:18–21)

The Parable of the Leaven

"He spoke another parable to them: 'The Kingdom of Heaven is like yeast which a woman took and hid in three measures of meal, until it was all leavened'" (Matthew 13:33 WEB).

This parable seems to refer to human activities throughout the earthly stage of the Church. Because leaven typifies sin in scripture, we must understand that corrupt human actions in the earthly Church throughout its existence can contaminate what began and was given pure. The best example of leaven as a symbol of sin can be seen in the celebration of Passover. The use of unleavened bread represents the desire of celebrants not to contaminate their hearts with sin, presenting themselves symbolically pure before God on this very traditional and sacred biblical feast.

Moreover, the Jewish sages understood that Moses received the highest divine revelation given to any human being at Sinai. They also knew that this revelation would reach all its divine splendor when the Messiah appeared. The problem was that this revelation gradually lost its purity over time, despite the efforts of genuinely outstanding Jewish rabbis and scholars. All this happened because of human activities in what the Divinity has given pure and perfect.

Perhaps the best testimony to these human activities are the many divisions and disagreements we find today in Christianity and Judaism. We do not agree on how to follow what God indicates and have created divisions for this reason. It is difficult to understand why we have so many differences, yet God is One.

Because of different ideas about how God handles His plan of redemption, divisions have arisen in Judaism's religious and secular aspects. Conservatives, Reformed, Hasidic, Messianic, Lubavitch, various Orthodox groups, and secular Judaism struggle to find the right path. Some think that the Messiah will be a political deliverer; others see Him as a perfect priest for all humankind or a true bearer of peace. For secular Judaism, the land is that Messiah of Israel who gives life to his people (Am Israel). There is also the concept that the Messiah is a process, and when it is completed, it will be administered by someone who will come from the house of David. For others, the restored state of Israel is the Messiah (Medinat Israel). As for some others, it is simple— "I don't care."

Well, it is the same for Christians. Human actions on what God gave correctly through his Son have caused the divisions. This imperfect human intervention has been gradually contaminating what is perfect. Since the last significant reform in Christianism— the one separated the Roman Catholic and Protestant churches— there have been continuously occurring "mini-improvements." This magna separation created even more fragmentations and different schools of interpretation and liturgy.

But, similar to what is taught in Judaism, the Christian Bible teaches us that all that pollution will be removed in a purge when the Messiah returns. It is then that the Kingdom of Heaven will be established in all fullness. Let's continue to analyze two more of this incredible and explicit teaching of the Lord Jesus. Let us remember that we are talking about the Church as it develops on earth.

The Parable of the Weeds

> He set another parable before them, saying, "The Kingdom of Heaven is like a man who sowed good seed in his field, but while people slept, his enemy came and sowed darnel weeds also among the wheat, and went away. But when the blade sprang up and produced grain, then the darnel weeds appeared also. The servants of the householder came and said to him, 'Sir, didn't you sow good seed in your

field? Where did these darnel weeds come from?'
"He said to them, 'An enemy has done this.' "The
servants asked him, 'Do you want us to go and
gather them up?' "But he said, 'No, lest perhaps
while you gather up the darnel weeds, you root up
the wheat with them. Let both grow together until
the harvest, and in the harvest time I will tell the
reapers, "First, gather up the darnel weeds, and bind
them in bundles to burn them; but gather the wheat
into my barn."''" (Matthew 13:24–30 WEB)

In this parable, we can see the dual personality of the earthly Church.
Wheat grows together with weeds known as darnel or tares. This
enemy plant looks like wheat but is actually a weed. It grew while
the workers were asleep. The Lord explained the future evil human
behaviors in the earthly Church. The wheat that was sowed last
represents the true sons of God, and the tares constitute the evil
ones, all before the harvest, under the same definitions as Christians.
Of course, this interpretation is from an outsider's point of view.

This teaching from a wise Jewish rabbi explains the deterioration
process of the earthly Church and, very well, the future at the end
of time for these evildoers. Tares is like a fifth column acting from
inside its army in favor of the enemy. This blend brings a lot of
confusion. What will happen to the outside observers if this strategy
even confuses the faithful fighting forces?

The Parable of Good and Bad Fishes in the Net

Again, the Kingdom of Heaven is like a dragnet
that was cast into the sea and gathered some fish
of every kind, which, when it was filled, fishermen
drew up on the beach. They sat down and gathered
the good into containers, but the bad they threw

away. So will it be at the end of the world. The angels will come and separate the wicked from among the righteous, and will cast them into the furnace of fire. There will be weeping and gnashing of teeth. (Matthew 13: 47–50 WEB)

This is my favorite for its simplicity but profound illustration; let's analyze it.

1- The word *church* is translated from the Greek *ekklesia*, which means a group of people who have been called or separated from others. In the same way, we can see the group of fish inside the net as a separate group from the others that were not caught inside.

   Note: When you throw a net into the sea, you do not catch all the fish that are there even though the intention is to trap as many as possible. We can say that this group of fish in the net is a group that has been set apart from the others. Well, that is an *ekklesia*. But let's see what happens next—inside the net are collected two different kinds of fishes.

2- Not all the fish inside the net will be approved. Using the Jewish term, not all of them are *kosher*.

3- There will be a purge in order to keep only the good fish and discard the others. There is a process that must happen before the purge is done. This process consists of two stages, and like every process, it takes time:

   1) The complete filling of the net.
   2) The pulling to the shore of the net.

4- Once the net is on the shore, the purge begins.

5- Once the purge is over, we can better understand what happened as we look back. The nature of the earthly Church was composed of a church within another church. The Church before the purge is not the final product.

How do we use the term *church*? It is a group of people who have been taken away from a larger group of people. In the case of the Church, it is a double process—the earthly cycle of the Church when the net was thrown and filed, and the spiritual or final approach when the good ones will be set apart. Note that God did indicate from the beginning who the real ones were, but that it needed to be in this way: "Let them both grow together until the harvest" (Matthew 13:30)

When we collect all the parables in this chapter, we have a great picture of the Kingdom of Heaven and its implementation on earth. This masterful narrative recorded in this chapter captures something fundamental that a Jewish rabbi (Jesus) taught to a very Jewish audience in a very Jewish context.

After analyzing this critical portion of the Christian side of the Bible, we can understand why sometimes the Jews have suffered persecution from within the worldly Christian Church.

We must analyze the teaching of Jesus again when He was asked about a premature purge:

> "No," he replied. "If you do that, you'll probably pull up the Wheat as well, while you're collecting the weeds. Let them both grow together until the harvest. Then, when it's time for harvest, I will give the reapers this instruction: First gather the weeds and tie them up in bundles to burn them but gather the wheat into my barn." (Matthew 13:29–30)

"Let them both grow together until the harvest." This is the actual stage we, the earthly Church, go through. It's the process we are immersed in right now. It is also the equivalent of the activity of completely filling and pulling the net to shore. As we may say, it is also the time before the purge and the harvest.

There are additional strong words of Jesus about this harmful human activity in the earthly and historical Church. Let's look at this one in His master discourse known as the Sermon of the Mount.

> "Not everyone who says to me, 'Lord, Lord,' will enter into the Kingdom of Heaven, but he who does the will of my Father who is in heaven. Many will tell me in that day, 'Lord, Lord, didn't we prophesy in your name, in your name cast out demons, and in your name do many mighty works?' Then I will tell them, 'I never knew you. Depart from me, you who work iniquity.'" (Matthew 7:21–23 WEB)

These are strong words from the Lord about the reprehensible attitude of some who claim to represent Christianity on earth. Perhaps some Christians will say that this is not the true Church. Precisely, this is the earthly or worldly Church. It is the Church before the purge! Its activities (good and bad) in this world have affected those who have been watching the Church from the outside. *But beware! As we have read, it is not for us to determine who is and who is not, although by our fruits we shall be known.*

Let's say something else about these words of Jesus. These are precisely some of the signs that Jesus said would accompany those who followed Him. "These signs will accompany those who believe in my name they will cast out demons; they will speak with new languages;[18] they will take up serpents; and if they drink any deadly thing, it will in no way hurt them; they will lay hands on the sick, and they will recover." (Mark 16:17-18 WEB)

So, what's the difference between these two kinds of signal makers? Possibly those rejected by the Lord are people who seek to enlarge themselves before the others claiming to be selected as "premium." They are in the spirit of Ananias and Sapphira—the opposite of Jesus's teachings! "It shall not be so among you; but whoever desires to become great among you shall be your servant" (Matthew 20:26 WEB).

Those who humbly recognize themselves as unworthy know that only the Messiah can save them; they never take credit for the signals that follow them. They give God all credit from their hearts.

Jesus himself rejected being described as One who excelled in human terms.[38] On some occasions, He worked miracles to benefit those in need; He asked them not to tell anybody. He hid from the people who wanted to establish him as king and Messiah in their human terms. Even the apostles rejected worldly worship[39] every time God manifested his power through them. The Christian sector of the Bible is full of these examples.

An outside observer may think that everyone inside the net and the field is part of that bad historical attitude, the kind of behavior credited to the earthly Church. The fish outside the net witnessed and judged every circumstance. These are dramatic words by Jesus.

CHARACTERISTIC 3: DUAL EFFECT

We have already seen that the Christian Church, in its earthly phase, has a dual personality. Also, we have discussed that, in the New Testament, the reason for that double standard is explained. But how will this dual personality of the earthly Christian Church affect its relationship with national Israel? Well, Moses prophesied that it would provoke Israel to anger and jealousy. This is one of the essential teachings of the Bible that has to do with the interrelationship between the Christian Church and national Israel.

Moses, in his farewell prophetic speech before his death, warned the Hebrew people about God's intentions to raise up another special nation. This was not to replace them with new people (see Statement 6); rather, it was to move them to jealousy and anger. These new people would have unique physical, geographical, and spiritual characteristics, which would make them different from the people of any other Gentile nation on earth. But who are these people?

Well, who else but the Christian Church? Paul devoted chapters 9 through 11 of his letter to the Church in Rome to explain the details of this conflict. Paul also gave us more information about this issue in almost all his letters.

Furthermore, who recognized a Jewish Messiah as king of the Universe? Is it not the Christian Church? Apart from Israel, who trusts the Jewish scriptures as given by God? Is it not the Christian Church? (This is explained at the beginning of this book in "A Brief Introduction to the Christian and Jewish Bibles and their Relationship.")

Which prophetic books does Christianity trust the most? Are they not those of the Jewish Bible? Whose martyrs have given their lives for a Messiah of Jewish origin and His message? Are they not the Christians? The Gospel was brought to earth by a Jewish Messiah, a message that was preached initially by His eleven original Jewish apostles. Has the Gospel not reached all the ends of planet Earth as commissioned? (Matthew 28:18–20). If it has not yet, soon it will. The effort is marching on, and nothing can stop it until it is completed.

Why does Israel have to be bothered by a strange nation that does not have the Jewish model as a reference? The only nation that is not a nation that insists on following a Jewish Messiah is the Christian Church in its entire earthly conflictive presence before the final purge. Let us see what Paul tells us about this face-to-face interaction: "But I say, did not Israel know? First Moses saith, I will provoke you to jealousy by them that are no people (ethnos), and by a foolish nation (ethnos) I will anger you" (Romans 10:19 KJV).

From where does Paul quote this scripture? Paul was quoting what is written in Deuteronomy 32:21. In light of the Gospel, he defines something that happened approximately fifteen centuries ago as told before; specifically, when Moses was about to die.

Moses saw the earthly Church. He saw its double personality

and its double effect on the Jewish Nation. Israel, said Moses, would be moved to jealousy and anger by these mysterious people. In his role as prophet, Moses spoke the following words from God to the Hebrew people: "They [Israel] have moved me to jealousy with that which is not God [idols]; they have provoked me to anger with their vanities [idolatry]: and I will move them to jealousy with those *which are not a people* [am]; I will provoke them to anger with a foolish [nabal] nation [goy]" (Deuteronomy 32:21 KJV)

In Moses's last speech, he warned the nation of Israel of a human group he did not describe as a nation (am) that would provoke them to jealousy. Note that Moses did not represent the human group that will provoke Israel to jealousy as Gentiles, but as a human group that is not a nation (am). Why is this? Well, *because these provokers of jealousy do not conform to the meaning that the Jewish people give to the expression* Gentiles. In the Bible and in its Jewish meaning, its definition is negative, relating them to almost nonhuman people—people far away from God.

Even Jesus emphatically used the term *Gentiles* for the nonbelievers (Matthew 10:5, Matthew 18:15–17). For the purpose of this analysis, we are going to stay with the Jewish and Bible definitions of the term *Gentiles*.[40] In addition, in Judaism, this term designates all non-Jewish human beings regardless of their nationality.

This concept also divides the human species into two groups—them and us. However, throughout time, when events have occurred in which some Gentile people have risked their lives to save the lives of Jews, the Hebrew nation, to recognize them, has added to the word *Gentile* the adjective *righteous*. That is why we can find the title "righteous among the nations" next to the name of some non-Jewish persons.

But that does not mean that Gentiles are far from the vital promises of God in the biblical message. On the contrary, in both Jewish and Christian scriptures, there has always been mention of a divine rescue for Gentiles who invoke the name of the God of

Abraham, Isaac, and Jacob.[41] This does not mean that the Jewish religious system must be adopted by non-Jewish followers of the God of Israel as I have discussed before.

About the foolish nation that would move Israel to anger—are they the same people who will provoke jealousy in Israel? We have to say yes and no at this moment in time. Yes, because Israel, for the moment, considers them to be the same human group. No, because the reality is that they are two distinct people no matter what they are seen as one. This human group provokes in Israel these two different reactions. Let us remember that the final purge that Jesus talked about with regard to His Church has not happened yet (Matthew 13:24–30, 44–50). See previous earthly Church characteristics.

In Deuteronomy 32:21, the human group that God will raise up to provoke Israel to *jealousy* is described neither as a nation (עַם - am), but not as Gentiles. Instead, the people who will move Israel to *wrath* are described as foolish (בְלָנ – nabal) Gentiles (גּי – goy).

Today, similar to the way it was in Paul's time, it may seem that they are the same human group from the Jewish point of view. Throughout the Old Covenant, the horrible connotation of the term Gentiles is continually emphasized. We have already spoken of how difficult it was for the first Jewish followers of Jesus to accept the Gentiles who came to the Church. (See Statement 5)

Let's go back again to the term *nation*. The Greek original ἔθνος (*ethnos*), used by Paul, means a group of people that, in an organic relationship, share common bonds, usually language, ancestry, religion, history, customs, and symbolism. These are mainly defined as a nation.

The next question is: What is not a nation? Well, the Christian Church is an excellent example of that. As a universal structure, the Church is composed of people of all epochs and different cultures, sometimes with huge differences. The Church is a body of believers who embrace different, cultures, languages or dialects, and various grades of civilization or technological knowledge. It is difficult to define the Church in what we mean by *nation*. But this is the one that Moses told his people that will provoke jealousy in them: "Now I will rouse their jealousy through people who are not a nation." Other Bible versions say, "a nation that is not a nation."

The Church comprises both definitions. The Church also fulfills the meaning of being a nation because we have the most important common bond, which goes far beyond culture. That is mutual faith in Jesus. This faith is much more than believing or belonging to any Christian denomination.

People have stolen the messianic figure of Jesus, gentilizing it and grotesquely robbing symbols and structures of Judaism while uprooting them from their real biblical significance and purpose are probably causing some jealousy and anger in the Jewish people. But when those things affect them in the name of Christianity, the situation worsens.

The rootedness and insistence in place for centuries on the part of countless Gentiles from among all nations in having a Jew as leader is challenging to some. Jesus was a Jew who presented himself to the Gentile world as its savior, identifying himself as the Messiah promised to Israel. This is something that requires much thought and consideration.

Many figures have already proclaimed themselves the Messiah, both in Judaism and in the Gentile world. Time and history have been responsible for unmasking them one by one. Only one has remained and prevailed again and again. This is Jesus! The fact is that countless Gentiles, continuously and throughout Church history, have found their Savior and Messiah in a Jew.

Gentiles who have shown a faith like Father Abraham, with many having offered their lives, might arouse some curiosity, jealousy, and even anger in the people who are still waiting for that messiah. Who are these people who proclaim a Jew to be their Messiah and Savior despite not being bonded by a shared history or nationality? Those people are the Church!

Throughout the history of the Church here on planet Earth,

some very outlandish preachers, teachers, and leaders have been responsible for the many outward criticisms that Christianity receives. These strange figures in the earthly Church have created an atmosphere of mocking around the figure of Jesus in some Jewish and Gentiles circles. Also, an "I don't care" attitude comes with rejection in others. Yet despite all that, the figure of Jesus remains immaculate, crisp, and pure as the redeemer of born-again believers as well as all those who, day by day, keep on discovering in a Jew, their Savior.

Throughout human history, nations have desecrated other nations, mainly because of fears, ambition, envy, or to rob their resources. Other times, cultural matters affect relationships between nations. But in this case, the main treasure in dispute is a figure, the desired one of the nations, the Messiah! Is Jesus the Messiah as the Church proclaims? Is this recognition of the messianism of Jesus, mainly by the Gentiles, which has already lasted for so many centuries, a cause for jealousy for some Jews? To whom does He belong? Who is correct about Him—Jews or Gentile believers?

On the matter of the Church that loves a Jewish Messiah so dearly, which provokes jealousy in some Jewish people, I think it may be very appropriate; this may be answered only by a Jewish person. Although I have had my own experiences about this, perhaps it may not be proper to go into them.

There is enough evidence throughout history about the anger that was caused by some religious christian cultures in the Jewish heart. In relatively recent times, the infamous Holocaust and the Russian pogroms are examples. In earlier times, the Spanish Inquisition, and the Crusades are examples. But the list is longer around the world. We can also consider the cultural and social facts and not just the religious issues about these events.

Alfredo Calderon-Rodriguez

INSERTION B: COMMENTARIES ON LUKE, THE ONLY NON-JEWISH CHRISTIAN BIBLE WRITER

Luke was the only non-Jewish writer of the Christian Bible, specifically. Despite not being Jewish, he was diligent and precise in investigating the facts he wrote in the Gospel that bears his name. In addition, he was the companion of the apostle Paul (Shaul) in his mission to spread the Gospel and an eyewitness to many things he covered in the book of Acts. Luke began both books by emphasizing the integrity of what he wrote.

> Since many have undertaken to set in order a narrative concerning those matters which have been fulfilled among us, even as those who from the beginning were eyewitnesses and servants of the word delivered them to us, it seemed good to me also, having traced the course of all things accurately from the first, to write to you in order, most excellent Theophilus; that you might know the certainty concerning the things in which you were instructed. (Luke 1:1–4 WEB)

> The first book I wrote, Theophilus, concerned all that Jesus began both to do and to teach, until the day in which he was received up, after he had given commandment through the Holy Spirit to the apostles whom he had chosen. To these he also showed himself alive after he suffered, by many proofs, appearing to them over a period of forty days, and speaking about God's Kingdom. (Acts 1:1–3 WEB)

Notice the meticulous investigation of Luke as a secondary author of the Bible, the only non-Jew among all Bible writers. John the apostle was very emphatic about placing himself as a personal witness on what he wrote, and Luke made it very clear that before he wrote, he did excellent research. Both trusted in their compilation of the events.

SOME WORDS FROM THE AUTHOR

I came to believe in Jesus after a breakdown in my life. Growing up in Puerto Rico, I felt lost in a Christian culture, mainly traditional Roman Catholic with a lot of Protestant influence. Questions like: Who am I? Why am I alive? What is life all about, and what is its purpose? Is God real? Does God exist? Is Jesus the Son of God? Does He love me as some people had told me, and why? Those and other questions and many disappointments at a very young age kept me in despair, even though I was blessed with good parents, siblings, family members, and friends. But looking around at the nonsense way of living that surrounded me, I came to a desperate search because I needed to find a purpose in life.

What was my next step? I looked for my landing zone in my efforts. I explored information about extraterrestrial beings, reading all sorts of books. Nothing! The topic was exciting, engaging, and full of possibilities, but there was no deep conviction of finding the truth. Emptiness and loneliness fully accompanied me.

The reality was that I wanted to meet with God. Somehow, deep in me, I believed in an origin and a purpose for being alive. But who sourced it and why? I decided then to choose to seek God.

I visited multiple Catholic and Protestant churches of different denominations. I investigated mediums, oriental philosophy, UFO mysteries, and other topics. I found nothing but more confusion. Some people from various denominations came to say that theirs was the true Church. This caused even more confusion! I asked myself which could be the real one out of the many cults, religions, and denominations. At this time, only one answer has come to me so far, and it came in the form of another question: If God is One, why are there so many divisions? So, it is better to look for the trunk and not consider the different branches.

The logic of this strategy was crucial because, if God exists and that He is good, as I had been told by so many, He will answer anyone who tries to approach Him honestly. So, I did it that way. As years passed by, having already set off, I discovered the truth of that intuition. Jesus Himself established that anyone who ran to Him would not be cast out (John 6:37).

So, I keep on struggling, but in a vital enterprise, searching for the meaning and purpose of my life! Looking for God!

Without going into small details, I will say that a New Testament came into my hands one day. Never before had I intended to read the Bible as a fountain of guidance. My idea of the Bible was that it is a mysterious book that not everyone can touch. It is a sacred book containing God's terrible Word. A text full of judgments and terrible punishments, something scary for me.

Anyway, in a long process, with some extraordinary experiences that guided me, I started reading the New Testament, beginning with the Gospel of Matthew. Interesting! For the first time in my life, I entered the Bible with curiosity and interest. Never had I the slightest suspicion that Matthew was a Levite, a Jewish tax collector, whose life was changed by Jesus's message and a firsthand witness of Him.

I devoured the New Covenant, but my life was still in trouble. I was hooked on alcoholism from my early youth when I was desperately trying to find a place to anchor my life. So many of my friends were the same way, so I had just followed.

Almost every week, for more than a year, I entered the woods in

El Yunque, a rain forest national park close to San Juan. Sometimes I went for hours and hours of hiking, walking, and thinking. I wanted to be alone with my quest, and one of the first things that struck me from the Bible was this verse: "Ask, and it will be given you. Seek, and you will find. Knock, and it will be opened for you" (Matthew 7:7 WEB). Wow! Words from Jesus direct to the human heart! "That's what I am looking for!" Immediately I told myself, "I want answers!" But later on, I realized that I had found much more than simple answers. Yes, I received a great response: "The Great I am." I had an encounter with the One who gives purpose to human life. I knocked, and a door was open for me, a door that connects to heaven.

A great and deep satisfaction sprang up in my heart the day I discovered that Jesus was what my soul was so much in need of. It was an experience that enveloped my whole being, spirit, soul, and body, and for the first time, I had the certainty in my heart that I had found what I had been looking for so earnestly.

But the good thing is that this is for everyone who seeks God honestly. That door is still open for humans who want to ask, search, and knock. They will get answers, find Jesus, and a wide-open door will be opened for them.

I'm also aware that it is impossible for any human who exists—except for Jesus in His earthly days (John 10:30, 14:9–10)—to know God deeply. In any book written about the God of the Bible, there will always be something incomplete, not well explained, or something that somebody else would explain better. That includes this book you are reading that I have written. This is because, after all, trying to understand the Only Eternal God takes an eternity.

But we should not worry, for God has given us that time with His presence. That is His gift to those who believe and trust in Him alone rather than in their own ways.

Forty-seven years later, I still have many questions, honestly. I still think that the Universe is full of surprises, but it also has a king—the King of kings. My questions are becoming answers, little by little, without haste. I have received the Great I Am for my inquiries, satisfaction, and patience. And in response to having knocked on the door, I have received a vast and frank entrance to His Kingdom. (It is undeserved; I received it just by grace.)

But why this connection with Israel? For a non-Jew by birth (who knows about my ancestors?), my interest may sound strange. I first went to Israel in 1980. For the first time in my life, I stood on one of the hills of Galilee. A deep, beautiful, inexplicable, and overwhelming feeling saturated my inner self in a surprising way. I was captured by an immense sensation that the purpose of my life was tied to what had happened there. It was as if I had been holding hands with hundreds of angels, connecting me through time to a distant past to which I belonged in that land. Somehow, I knew I had finally come home! Wow! Please, don't ask any more questions; I still can't explain it.

Well, I think there are other very relevant matters that may explain that connection; let's see:

1- My savior was born a Jew. God provided His Son to be our atonement.
2- The giver of the message of salvation was a Jew.
3- The Jewish and Christians scriptures guarantee that He is the One we should seek.
4- The first members of the church were all Jewish.
5- The apostle commissioned to reach out for us, the non-Jews, was Jewish.
6- The Holy Bible was elaborated through Jewish or Israeli hands on approximately 97%. (2 books credited to Luke, the only Gentile of the Bible writers, out of 66 in the Protestant compilation. 100% - (2/66) = 97%)
7- The roots of my faith are Jewish.
8- I'm grafted in the Natural Olive (Israel), and its roots nourish me.
9- The New Covenant is for Israel, and I joined in.

10- The promises of the God of Israel are mine too.

11- The prophets of Israel were the ones who foretold our Messiah.

12- The Jewish people paid a high price for this role (voluntarily or not).

People from all nations of the world are invited to join His kingdom. There are no rejections for those who want to get closer to Him. Jesus declares this: "All those whom the Father gives me will come to me. He who comes to me I will in no way throw out" (John 6:37 WEB). In the Kingdom of God, entrance is granted to those who, in their hearts, claim the Son, no matter their nationality. God Himself will welcome His redeemed ones.

Blessings to you all!

> Yea, many people and strong nations shall come to seek the Lord of hosts in Jerusalem, and to pray before the Lord. Thus saith the Lord of hosts; In those days it shall come to pass, that ten men shall take hold out of all languages of the nations, *even shall take hold of the skirt of him that is a Jew, saying, We will go with you: for we have heard that God is with you.* (Zechariah 8:22–23 KJV, emphasis mine)

> For Zion's sake will I not hold my peace, and for Jerusalem's sake I will not rest, until the righteousness thereof goes forth as brightness, and the salvation thereof as a lamp that burns. (Isaiah 62:1 KJV)

> For I could wish that I myself were accursed from Christ for my brothers' sake, my relatives according to the flesh who are Israelites; whose is the adoption, the glory, the covenants, the giving of the law, the service, and the promises; of whom are the fathers,

> and from whom is Christ as concerning the flesh,
> who is over all, God, blessed forever. Amen.
> (Romans 9:3–5 WEB)

Who Is Jesus?

Who is Jesus? If we try to define Jesus, we find it to be an impossible task. How many books do we already have addressed this daunting challenge? Countless. In the last two verses of John's Gospel, we read: "This is the disciple who testifies about these things and wrote these things. We know that his witness is true. There are also many other things which Jesus did, which if they would all be written, I suppose that even the world itself wouldn't have room for the books that would be written" (John 21:24–25 WEB).

These words of John are so up to date because of all that Jesus has continued doing. The actual existing literature about Him, and that which is still in production, is immense. Moreover, this monumental undertaking is gigantic proof of the universal importance of a Jew raised in the region of Galilee. This, among many other characteristics, undoubtedly separates Jesus from so many other self-proclaimed messiahs. Where are these false christ's? They have simply been fading away while the figure of Jesus has remained growing amid every tongue, people, and nation.

For two millennia, all who comprehend Jesus are being attacked in a thousand different ways, from the persecution and death of his followers to the mockery and scorn in more sophisticated circles. No area of human endeavor has been free from such persecution. But, even from all sectors of persecution, followers of Jesus are still coming out day after day. Why? Have they found the truth? This is a good question to try to answer.

Of the many things that can be said, and of those that have already been said about the figure of Jesus, let us look briefly at this Jesus's statement before Pilate: "Pilate therefore said to him, 'Are you a king then?' Jesus answered, 'You say that I am a king. For this reason, I have been born, and for this reason I have come into the world, that I should testify to the truth. Everyone who is of the truth listens to my voice.' Pilate said to him, 'What is truth?'" (John 18:37–38 WEB).

Jesus, at His trial overseen by Pilate, told the Roman governor that he had come to testify about the truth. Pontius Pilate's answer came in the form of a rhetorical question: "What is truth?" So, charged with indifference and contempt for the truth, Pilate ended his conversation with Jesus with this expression. This was bad for Pilate; if he had continued to talk to Jesus, Jesus would have replied: "I am the Truth." Of course, Pilate's life could have changed forever. Sadly, like Pilate, many people still evade a deep conversation with Jesus through the Bible.

In our modern times, humanity is confused by so much information that comes to us from so many different sources and interests. Information management has become one of the most dangerous activities of humanity. Every government in the world has intelligence departments, counterintelligence, and counter-counterintelligence agencies. We no longer know what the truth is or who to believe.

The field of conspiracy theories resembles a game of table tennis as information comes to one player as the ball with a lot of misleading effects, to be returned in the same way to the counterpart. This information rebound ends when one or more players succumb to a material so toxic and contaminated that it is no longer the truth. In this actual painful war between Ukraine and Russia, every piece of information that comes to us must be impartial and carefully debunked to be as close to the truth as possible.

But what is truth? In this world so accustomed to relativism, each "truth" is a particular way of seeing and understanding life. Should truth be divided into infinite fragments of relativity or subjectivity? Could each of these specific truth capsules be classified as truth? Or is the truth absolute? How does this relate to Jesus's words when he declared himself to be the Truth. What does all this mean?

Let's look at some main features of truth.

1- It is absolute. It sustains itself and sustains all things. Truth is perfect, no more and no less, and it will guide those who honestly seek it. Jesus also said of himself to be the Way (John 14:6, Isaiah 35:8–10).

2- It is eternal. It is always existing. Nothing can come out of the nonexistent. Nothingness does not exist because something exists. Nothing that exists today could be if it hadn't been something before. What was before has to be uncreated because there was nothing behind creating what always is. The always existing is the primary of all that is. That is why we are, and everything is (Colossians 1:16).

3- It is transcendent. It always was, always is, and always will be. It has no beginning because the truth has always been eternal to give place to what is and will be. It has no end because it cannot return to non-existence, for non-existence has no place when something exists. It is alpha and omega, enclosing our entire frame of reference in an eternal cycle of renewal and advancement. (Revelation 1:8).

Jesus was entirely sure of who He was and that He came to bear witness to the truth when He was on our planet for the first time. He did not only declare that he had come to bear witness to the truth, but said of himself, "I am the Truth." No respected world leader, religious or philosophical, has ever dared to declare such a statement. Only Yeshua!

If you want to know more about Jesus, just seek Him with your heart. For sure, you will find Him (Matthew 7:7). All His glory and splendor will be seen by every creature when He returns to earth: "Behold, he is coming with the clouds, and every eye will see him, including those who pierced him" (Revelation 1:7 WEB).

SECTION 4

CLOSING WORDS

W<small>HAT IS RELIGION</small>? I<small>T IS</small> the human effort to please what we perceive as the supreme of all things, whether one or several deities or the exaltation of our collectible or personal human ego.

Like other religions or faiths among humankind, the Christian faith is discerned by a sacred book, the Bible. As we can see from this analysis, the reason for this fervor against the Jewish nation in some Christian circles or cultures never comes from the message contained in the Christian Bible. In any case, it may be a personal and accommodative interpretation to justify certain feelings. As somebody once told me, "You can use the Bible to justify any sort of behavior." The problem with this way of thinking is that you can destroy that hypothesis with a straightforward question: Does the Bible justify your behavior?

Of course, the Jewish nation, like any other nation, is not perfect. Neither is the Church perfect while in this world. But Israel has had an essential role in God's plans, not because they deserve it, like any other Gentile nation, but because the promises that have been given to them were made by someone who will never fail to keep them. God Himself made those promises! It is very reasonable to understand that nation of Israel still will have a new era in the future with God's anointed One.

The author of Hebrews, in chapter 6 verse 13, begins to analyze the passage in Genesis 22:16–18 with these words: "For when God made a promise to Abraham, since he could swear by no one greater, he swore by himself" (WEB). When we read Hebrews 6:13–20, Genesis 12:1–3 and 22:16-18, we find that God's promises to Abraham included people from all nations of the earth.

What was the reason for God's compromise with Abraham? Indeed, it was because of Abraham's faith and trust in God. "Yahweh's angel called to Abraham a second time out of the sky, and said, "'I have sworn by myself,' says Yahweh, 'because you have done this thing, and have not withheld your son, your only son'" (Genesis 22:15–16 WEB)

What an image! It perfectly shows us the picture of redemption. Because of his father's faith, Isaac (the son of promise) was replaced by a Lamb provided by God. Today, by that same kind of faith, all of humanity can be part of this promise that will one day be fulfilled. In the meantime, there is hope. The Lamb of God has already been provided. According to the promise, provision has been made for all the children of Abraham (see Statement 3).

The gates of heaven are still wide open for all who seek the Seed of Abraham with all their hearts. God has provided a Lamb for His atonement! The old invitation is still new!

> There is no one like you among the gods, Lord, nor any deeds like your deeds. All nations you have made will come and worship before you, Lord. They shall glorify your name. (Psalm 86:9–10 WEB)

> Oh come, let's worship and bow down. Let's kneel before the Lord, our Maker, for he is our God. We are the people of his pasture, and the sheep in his care. Today, if you would hear his voice. (Psalm 95:6–7 NHEB)

ACKNOWLEDGMENT

To Jesus, the Author and Perfecter of our faith, hoping that everything contained in this book will bless someone in getting closer to God. To my dear Spouse, daughter, grandchildren, and son-in-law. To my brothers, sisters, nephews, and nieces, and to my family and the excellent friends by whom I have been so blessed. To the magnificent Jewish nation, my Jewish friends, and all people from other nations, cultures, and tongues on our beautiful planet.

I want to give thanks also for the innumerable good Pastors, Bible Teachers, and Preachers. For more than 47 years, those have nourished my soul with their tender love for God. To all fellow believers for being so great.

I am grateful for thousands Sunday Bible Schools that I have been a part of for many years. The encouragement, corrections, and good feelings from those others helped me overcome difficult times. For Christ-Bible-centered books that have helped me grow in spiritual matters. For the Bible studies and the incredible Body of Christ, the Church, the body that I belong. God bless us all.

CREDITS

Illustrations by Daniela Rolón and Photoshop edited by the author.

Front and back Cover art and design by Christian Feliciano.

NOTES

[1] In some Christian circles, the Old Testament is almost an exciting, wordy fossil to be studied only for historical reasons. In other Christian theological circles, it is an essential component that contains much currently vital information. We can easily harmonize the teachings of the Apostle Paul and Jesus related to this: The best and simplest way we have to understand this is to see how Jeremiah describes the change from the Old to the New Covenant. "I will write my laws in their minds and hearts." Notice that these are not new laws; they are the same but applied differently. In the New Covenant, they are no longer external ordinances and cultic rites to be blindly and unfaithfully accomplished. Now is the perfect divine justice comprehended in the Law given to Moses, forming part of the profound reality of the human heart. In other words, it is no longer something external but internal; it is the righteousness of God residing by His Spirit in the heart and mind of the redeemed soul. This is possibly what Jesus was referring to when he taught "I tell you until heaven and earth pass away, not even one smallest letter or one tiny pen stroke shall in any way pass away from the Law until all things are accomplished" (Matthew 5:18 WEB). This final part of the sentence, "until all things are accomplished," refers to when the human heart receives by faith in the redemptive work of Jesus on the cross, all the divine righteousness found in the Law of Moses as well as when all things are accomplished in God's redemption plans. Apostle Paul spoke of the cessation of the Law as something that had already fulfilled its purpose. Still, he was not speaking of the annulment of the righteousness of the Law but of its ritual application to obtain salvation. The apostle simply said that works of the Law cannot save us because of our inability to fulfill it (Romans 10:1–10). For this reason, he said that the Law was good, but

we are evil, sold under sin (Romans 7, 8:1–8). We see more of this topic in Statement 7

2   Jesus comprehended the human heart like no one ever had (John 2:23–25). Jesus knew that the origin of the confrontations he continually faced came from the failed condition of human nature—love for the darkness, religious hypocrisy, envy, jealousy, the imposition of interpretations on mosaic concepts that no one could fulfill, and fear of losing control over people are some issues that Jesus confronted. However, above all, perhaps he confronted the aversion to exposing the exact design of their hearts. Their self-projection as superior to others made them hide behind a legalism devoid of love for those in need. Those were the points that Jesus impacted with his simple answers. No one could resist that! When confronted with religious matters, Jesus went directly to human heart conditions. Read Matthew 15, Mark 21, Luke 6:45, and so many other passages of the Christian Bible. More about this in Statement 6.

3   Some theologians see an even more significant division in the methods of God's administration of His redemption plans. They call this school of interpretation dispensationalism. There are seven different stages or dispensations in the way God manages His redemption activities to rescue humankind. Maybe some people may think of this as an old way of theology; however, it is an excellent tool that helps to see all things in their space and time context and how God's redemption plans move forward over time.

4   It is in this responsibility that most Christian theologians agree that Israel as a nation fails partially. Paul, the apostle, explained this very clearly in his epistle to the Romans, not pointing to Israel as a sole scapegoat but bonding Gentiles and Jews in the same responsibility. Exodus 19:5–6 mentions the priestly mission of the Hebrew people to the nations. In this particularity, some Christian theologians think that Israel failed primarily. Nevertheless, the reality is that they could not fulfill their part of the covenant, as verse 5 says: "if you keep my covenant." The divine Law is too high for any human being to fulfill. We will discuss this interesting subject further in Statement 7.

5   It is a fact that the Jewish scriptures (Old Covenant) are a product solely of Jewish secondary authors. Secondary authors, because God Himself is the primary author who gave the true inspiration to the human writers. The New Covenant is also a product of secondary Jewish hands. Luke was the only non-Jewish writer of any of the Bible books. There is an addition at the end of the book that details this point more.

6   Other cultures and religions exist that have developed some versions of a messiah to come. Also, there have been many false messiahs appearing from time to time. However, before His arrival, Jesus was the only one foretold in previous scriptures. Only one has fulfilled so many written signs centuries before his first appearance. Only one has accomplished such extraordinary events and said that He would return. There is that much information in the Bible about the signals that Jesus accomplished that anyone who wants to know more may do proper research. Finally, at the end of Jesus's earthly life, He proved that He was the one to be expected, with His resurrection in front of many firsthand witnesses. (See 1 Corinthians 15:1–8, among many others Bible passages.)

7   Notice that the Church is composed of people from all epochs and nations. Notice, too, that all of the first followers of Jesus were Jews. So, it is not a matter that God abandoned the Jews to build a new nation for Him.

8   God never will contradict Himself because all of God's promises are in Him Yes, and in Him Amen. (2 Corinthians 1:20, Deuteronomy 7:9, Hebrews 6:13–18, Numbers 23:19, Habakkuk 2:3–4). The time for the complete fulfillment of some of God's promises is still in the future. It does not matter that there has been some partial fulfillment in times past. These are known as double reference prophecies. The best example of this is God's promises of total peace for the nation of Israel once they were installed in the promised land. History has let us know that, far from absolute peace, once the people of Israel came to settle in the Promised Land, there has been conflict after conflict to this day. So, we may ask, Where is this promised perfect peace? By faith, we know that it will happen when the Messiah reigns. For many, this will be at His return; for others, for the moment, it will be at His first coming. Hebrews 3:7–4:11 speaks of the perfect time of rest that is yet ahead for those who have lived by faith and those who currently live by faith in the Lord.

9   In this period, the roles are inverted. Quoting Paul again, this is when the Church struggles to obey, and Israel as a nation is in total rejection of Jesus as their Messiah (John 1:11–12). This is not to say that all Jews reject Jesus, but they, as a human group, in their national context, do. But hold on! There was mercy before for the Gentiles, and there is mercy now for the Jews. "For God has bound everyone [Jews and Gentiles] over to disobedience so that he may have mercy on them all" (Romans 11:32 WEB). More on this interesting fact in Statement 6.

10   Obedience in italic emphasis means only partial observance of God's requirements. Both human groups, Jewish and Gentiles, fail to be perfectly obedient to God.

11   Matthew 4:1–17, Mark 1:1–15, Luke 4:1–14.

12   Acts 9:21–22.

13   Galatians 2:1–9, Ephesians 2:1–22, 1 Timothy 3:16.

14   Acts 2:16, 25.

15   Romans 1:16.

16   Acts 5:36–37.

17   Acts 15:7,14.

18   Although there are different non-Jewish nationalities mentioned in the New Testament, they are all generally treated within the term Gentiles; in other words, us and them.

19   There are several passages in the New Testament from Luke, Paul, and Peter that mention that Jesus is that Rock on which His Church stands. That Rock is the foundation on which the Church now is planted. Peter was the first of Jesus's disciples to understand that powerful truth. We can find that event registered in Matthew 16:16–19. The truth revealed to Peter was that Jesus was the Messiah, the Son of God, who came to redeem Jews and Gentiles. Luke wrote in Acts 4:11. Paul wrote in 1 Corinthians 3:11, 10:4 and Ephesians 2:20. Finally, Peter wrote in 1 Peter 2:4–8. It is also good to look at Peter's speeches as recorded by Luke in the book of Acts: Acts 2:14–41; 3:1–6, 12–26; 4:8–12; 5:29–30. In these Bible passages, we can see how important and bold Peter's role was in the birth of Jesus Church.

20   Acts 11:19–26.

21   The Jewish Bible was the Bible that Jesus and the first believers read, quoted, and used for their preaching and teachings. The Christian part of the Bible was formed later. The Word of the Gospel was being spread, taught, and shared through apostles' letters and presential visits to the newly formed congregations of believers. From a selection of these letters, the New Testament developed. In this testament, the Jewish apostles established the fundamentals and interpretations of the Old Testament (Jewish scriptures or Tanah) that we as Christians have today.

22   Acts 18:6, Romans 11:13, Galatians 2:7–9.

23   John 8:3–11.

24   Mark 12:13–17. Jesus never hid when He was questioned by those who rejected Him. He usually was confronted with difficult matters of the Law of Moses. Still, He always answered with firmness, security, simplicity,

and a lot of wisdom. Other interesting examples are these: The Messiah is the son of David; Matthew 22:41–46; the entire chapter 12 of Matthew contains some Jesus fascinating conversations with His detractors.

25 Matthew recorded this interaction of Jesus in the temple with the multitude, the Pharisees, and Sadducees starting from Cap 21 and verse 23. This event ends at 23:39.

26 Ephesian 2:11–19. There were and there are numerous witnesses of Jesus's resurrection; it was not only witnessed by the apostles.

27 John 1:29–34.

28 That means that institutional, cultural, or religious Christianity, is just like any other religion on earth. In the second section of this book, we will see Jesus giving a Jewish audience a full description of the nature of the Christian Church on earth.

29 During the life and ministry of Jesus, He was constantly confronted, especially by religious leaders and their followers. Although not all confronted Him; some political and religious authorities came to Him for spiritual guidance (Mark 5:22–43, John 3:1-2). Jesus's message always emphasized the needs of the weakest. The proclaimed self-righteousness of these leaders was constantly shaken by the teachings of Jesus, especially when it came to loving one's neighbor (Matthew 23:23). Today, His word continues to confront every self-righteous heart and comfort the souls of all who hunger and thirst for justice.

30 Revelation 5:9.

31 Luke 24:27,44; John 1:45; Acts 28:23.

32 Deuteronomy 32:21.

33 Hebrews 11:13, 39–40.

34 1 John 1:1 is a classic declaration of thousands of people that walked, touched, listened to, or were affected by Jesus in many ways during His earthly days.

35 John 17:20. The Gospel has reached almost every corner of the world by the word that was spread by those first believers, firsthand witnesses of Jesus's ministry. Jesus, after His resurrection, met with eleven of His disciples in the Galilee region (Matthew 28:16–20). He gave them the great commission to reach the ends of the world with the good news of salvation. Everything began with just eleven persons. But Jesus did not send them by themselves; He empowered them with a new baptism, the anointing of His constant presence in the Spirit (Acts 1:6–11).

36 1 Peter 1:6–9, 2 Timothy 4:7, Hebrews 12:1–2.

37 Russell Moore, "The church is the gathering of these strangers and aliens (Church members); it's the outpost (on earth) of Gods' kingdom." Onward, Engaging the Culture Without Losing the Gospel, page 24.

38 John 6:11–15. There are many others Bible passages that show that Jesus tried to evade publicity; He did not come to receive notoriety in human religious terms, but to save humankind.

39 Acts 14:8–18. This is not the only passage in which a member of the Church rejected personal recognition from the people mainly after sharing the good news of the Gospel with them. We can also see the different approaches of the people and the mixed feelings or syncretism they tried to bring in when attracted by Jesus's message. That is why Jesus was so adamant to keep His message pure. This also defines the real character of the Church.

40 The word *Gentile* can have two meanings. In secular terms, it can go from negative to neutral to positive; it depends on the context in which it appears. But in the Bible, and in its Jewish meaning, the definition is negative, suggesting Gentiles were almost non-human people, people far away from God, like a bunch of animals. (Strong H1471)

41 In the promise of Abraham, all the families of the earth were included. Jonas the prophet was sent to the Gentile city of Nineveh. Also see Isaiah 11:10, 42:6, 60:3–5 and Malachi 1:11 among others Bible passages. God also designated the apostle Paul to be in a special ministry to the Gentiles.

Printed in the United States
by Baker & Taylor Publisher Services